TO THE

ICE

AND BEYOND

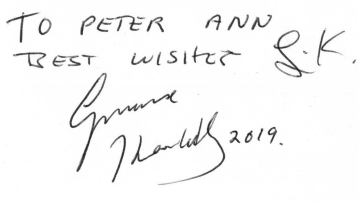

TO PETER ANN
BEST WISHES G.K.

Graeme
Thowlins 2019.

TO THE

ICE
AND BEYOND

KIWI YACHTSMAN'S EPIC SOLO CIRCUMNAVIGATION VIA THE ARCTIC NORTHWEST PASSAGE

GRAEME KENDALL

MARY EGAN
PUBLISHING

Dedicated to Eileen and Harold

Published by Mary Egan Publishing
www.maryegan.co.nz

Published 2016
Reprinted 2017

© Graeme Kendall
www.iceandbeyond.com
gk@astralexpress.com

The right of Graeme Kendall to be identified as the author of this work in terms
of section 96 of the Copyright Act 1994 is hereby asserted.

Designed and produced by Mary Egan Publishing
Cover designed by Anna Egan-Reid and Stephanie Van Oijen
Printed in China

ISBN 978-0-473-39906-1

CONTENTS

FOREWORD

I was delighted when Graeme asked me to write this foreword, as it gave me a good reason to become immersed in his book and to ponder further just what it is that creates and rewards the solo sailor.

The only other solo sailor I have really talked to was Adrian Hayter, our sailing instructor at Outward Bound in the Marlborough Sounds at the top of the South Island, New Zealand, back in February 1963 and the first man to sail solo from the United Kingdom to New Zealand. Adrian struck me as a person who was used to risk and was quite undeterred by it.

He thought we students should be sailing the whalers across Cook Strait, a famously turbulent stretch of water separating the two main islands of New Zealand. I asked what would happen if there was a storm. "Just run before it," he said. So I said, "How about three days later when you are 500 miles into the Pacific?" "No problem," he said, "as long as you have enough food."

I have to say I got plenty enough excitement as a 16-year-old just sailing the whaler in 50 knots of wind as we left Ship Cove and headed towards Anakiwa, a mere 70 kilometres through Queen Charlotte Sound, and have never had the slightest urge to sail offshore on my own.

Graeme's book, written frankly in the first person, goes a long way to answering questions about what it takes to be a successful solo sailor.

Imagine setting out on a 28,000-mile journey with no fridge or water maker, only a 140-litre tank and several bottles of emergency water. There is no doubt that proper planning, which prevents poor performance, was a feature of the entire escapade. As someone who normally remembers a forgotten item when driving away from the house, I am impressed that Graeme planned and executed his mission without one missing item.

I liked the brief conversation when someone asked what he was doing and he said, "Planning a trip around the world," and the next question was, "And what else?"

"And what else?" shows that most of us, and I have to include myself, have no real grasp of what constitutes proper planning for a voyage of this scale.

To travel such a distance alone is an extraordinary feat, and Graeme did it by focusing each day on the next step. In a voyage that was always planned to start and end at the same point, he exemplifies the notion that "the journey is what matters".

And in this way the story of his life – his journey – and especially the part told in this book becomes a tutorial from which we can all of us learn. In many ways, it's a "how to", and will reward people who highlight passages.

And in amongst the detail of life, sailing and planning, you find nuggets of philosophy, even wisdom, and the sum of these creates a picture and helps explain what drove Graeme to and through this remarkable adventure.

I like his use of visualisation, and the various notes about ageing, in which he considers his own body as just another piece of equipment to maintain and look out for.

You also get a strong sense that Graeme views the rest of his life as if time is precious indeed and wasting it a real mistake.

I found it very interesting that he got 55 knots of wind on his first night out, and that he needed to average 150 miles a day to get to the

Northwest Passage entrance by the end of August. The first speaks volumes about his confidence when departing, and the second that he was happy to give the whole trip a real urgency. Others might be tempted to put a few weeks up their sleeves, but not Graeme.

"I was always conscious of my timetable and the need to keep pushing on," he writes.

There is no sense of regret in that statement, rather the opposite, as if it gave him a welcome sense of purpose always.

By the time he got across the Tasman and Coral Sea and inside the Barrier Reef, he was 10 miles per day down on this average, and needed to keep the pressure on.

The book is full of little treasures, such as his encounter with 20 migrating birds, and in fact birds are a feature of his journey through-out and were sorely missed when he was truly alone in the Beaufort Sea.

I was intrigued by Graeme's daily catch-up with himself over a rum and coke, where he revisited the day, and his plan, and went forward with a renewed purpose.

That habit would work I am sure for people in all sorts of activity, whether group or individual.

There is a story I heard once that illustrates Graeme's winning attitude. He ran a car dealership in Christchurch and was taking a Rolls Royce for a run when he got pulled over by a traffic policeman for some real or suspected infringement. After the necessary formalities and before saying goodbye, Graeme asked the officer, "Have you ever driven a Rolls?"

It turned out the answer was no, so Graeme asked, "Well, would you like to have a drive of this one?" And the answer to that was yes.

I am sure they departed on good terms and that really sums up Graeme's dealings with people throughout his life and throughout this book. His life is a journey in which most of the interactions are win-win.

Like Hayter and, I suspect, most of the other soloists, Graeme has his share of confidence and there are several episodes in this book where he takes the more bullish option while on the water. Yet one fact that shines through is that Graeme is definitely not a naïve dreamer. He is very experienced on the ocean and knew his boats, even before he began investigating this journey.

He is at home on the sea, not just as a cruiser but also as an ocean racer.

His journey approaching Cape Agulhas reads as pure magic, and makes one want to go to sea, as does the connection with the giant sea turtle, two green flashes and the birds at Diomede Island in Bering Strait.

Graeme, who is such a communicative individual, states that he wouldn't have contemplated the voyage without knowing that there could be constant communication with family, friends – teammates, really.

Occasional quotes open windows into the full experience – "but I was lonelier in the hotel than I had been on the boat".

All in all, this is a book to be savoured, to be read time and again.

—Tom Schnackenberg

Tom Schnackenberg is synonymous with yacht-racing innovation and success. He has been involved in 12 America's Cup campaigns, including designing sails for Australia II, the yacht that in 1993 took the cup away from the US, and was design co-ordinator and navigator for New Zealand's successful 1995 and 2000 campaigns. In 2003 he headed the Team New Zealand syndicate.

A physicist with strong ties to the University of Auckland, Tom brought sails into the computer age, adding new designs and new ways of testing, such as the Twisted Flow Wind Tunnel which simulates the winds to see how sails behave. He is a member of the America's Cup Hall of Fame.

PROLOGUE

The ice was here, the ice was there,
The ice was all around:
It cracked and growled, and roared and howled,
Like noises in a swound!
—Samuel Coleridge, "The Rime of the Ancient Mariner"

I stood alone in the cockpit of *Astral Express*, peering into the fog. To the west, in the invisible distance, the vertical slopes of Baffin Island plunged into the sea. At this latitude, most of North America sprawled behind me, to the south and west. Greenland's icy wastes lay some 125 miles to the east.

At around 73 degrees north, and well inside the Arctic Circle, I had reached the ice edge. For three days I'd been sailing around icebergs, but now ahead was a stretching field of thickening ice. It was about five in the morning, daylight in the fleeting Arctic summer, but fog pressed around me, drawing a grey veil over the world a couple of hundred metres ahead. A silent world, apart from the cold sea lapping at my boat. But underneath me now, ice roared across my keel.

Sea ice. Most of the ice in the Arctic is this, frozen seawater. When it freezes in a calm sea it's nice and flat, and easy to traverse. But as the wind increases and the seas build up, the pieces crash together, tipping and pushing against each other so that they rise up to form a jagged, mountainous terrain – an ever-changing landscape.

I had reduced sail and was meandering into the white, giving myself time to figure out the best way through. A strange smell hung in the air. I proceeded cautiously through the fog.

Unlike icebergs, which form from glaciers in the valleys of the land, sea ice conducts its lifecycle in the ocean, forming once the water temperature reaches about minus three degrees. More buoyant than freshwater ice, because of the pockets of brine trapped in its structure in its initial stages, sea ice is always on the move – a floating mass that shifts with the direction of the wind and currents, until it congests into immense blockades in bays and tight areas. It builds up over years and can be many metres thick, although this stuff that *Astral Express* was nosing into was more like two or three. Flat, broken sea ice can be easy to push through, whereas disturbed and congested ice is heavier and harder to move. Also, as the ice moves through the years, it hardens. The brine drains away, and ice that's been around for up to four winters is very hard.

Another hour and I was in heavy ice trying to find my way through this maze while edging further east. If it wasn't for the fog I could have climbed up the mast for a view forward but as it was there was little to see.

I had ice charts from the Canadian Ice Service, the most recent just two days old. It showed this ice field, and it revealed two ways of avoiding it. I could sail out to the east, then north and back around to Lancaster Sound; or I could stay on this more westerly course toward the northern shore of Baffin Island where it looked as if there was a lead, an open stretch of water close to the shore that would allow me to cut straight on up to Lancaster. I was tempted by the shorter distance offered by the lead. I made estimations based on what I knew about the ice field's movement and melt, and thought it would have shrunk in the interim. Yes, I decided, it looked pretty open.

The surface freezes first and fast, but there's four times as much ice under the water as there is on top and it was this invisible base that *Astral Express* was now catching. The noise of ice against hull or keel is tremendous and at first disconcerting. The boat acts like a drum and to begin with you're sure the boat must be damaged. Down below, it's almost deafening as the jagged ice slides past.

The wind was between five and eight knots. I had the headsails furled and with just the mainsail up I could control my speed. I sailed slowly on, thinking I was heading into the lead.

I had been here before. Five years earlier I got almost this far – up through the Labrador Sea, through the Davis Strait and into Baffin Bay, just a day and a half from Lancaster Sound, the entrance point for the fabled Northwest Passage. But that year the passage was closed – the fierce, capricious Arctic winds had blown ice down from the north, blocking the entrance and thwarting my ambition. There was nothing for it but to turn back. There are many things in life you can control, but Arctic weather is not one of them.

This time it was looking pretty good. Lancaster Sound seemed clear, according to the reports of the Canadian Ice Service. But I still had to get there.

However, instead of shrinking, the lead was filling up with ice. *Astral Express* had a bow of Kevlar. She was, literally, bulletproof. But she wasn't an ice breaker. She could push through slushy, small ice. She was okay hitting the odd piece by accident, but generally I tried to avoid it completely. Now, though, it was getting worse.

On a large flat piece of ice, maybe 100 metres long and 15 high at its highest point, I passed a group of about 30 seals resting, black against the white ice. I was perhaps just 10 to 15 metres away from them. That explained the smell.

And just after that, the ice massed into platforms and lumps there was no hope of pushing through. Finally, my bow wedged into the icy vice formed by two craggy piles, each three metres high, and there was no way forward. Below me, the keel ground on ice. My mouth went dry.

There's no good outcome to getting stuck in the ice up here. The window of opportunity for getting through the Northwest Passage, where I was bound, is two to four weeks. That's all you've got when the ice has melted enough to allow a passage through – and that's if you're lucky. Often, even within that window of opportunity, the wind pushes the ice into impassable bottlenecks. And once that few weeks is over, the freeze gets its grip again and the ice quickly grabs hold of the sea. Soon, too, the darkness comes – a relentless, frozen darkness that has literally driven men mad. Polar bears pace the ice, their acute sense of smell attracted by cooking smells.

I had a gun, and a yacht that was coated in Kevlar. *Astral Express* was unlikely to get crushed by the pressure of the gathering ice. Perhaps I could fight off a polar bear. But I didn't want to spend a winter on the ice. It was time to get out of there. As *Astral Express* ground to a halt, I grabbed the pole and began pushing.

My frantic attempts to clear the boat from the ice were a whirl of movement in the silent, remote landscape. I could hear my own breath, and the crunching of the pole on the ice. The water was crystal clear and calm and I could see the ice below that the keel was hitting. Desperately I pushed, first one side then the other, and finally, almost imperceptibly at first, we began to loosen against the ice. After more pushing I was clear enough that I could turn the boat around even though she was still touching the ice underneath.

I still had the mainsail up, but I had it feathered into the wind during the time I was stuck so that it wouldn't fill. Then once I'd managed to turn, I reset it so I could make my way again. This was possible only because of the light wind – if it had been any stronger I'd have needed to reef the mainsail or drop it altogether and reset it once I was back on course.

It took about an hour until I was clear enough to find a pathway out of there, back the way I had come. Fortunately, because the wind was light, the ice hadn't blown around much since I'd come in so I could follow my own track in reverse, thanks to my GPS screen. I couldn't have done it visually. There was no obvious trail through this foggy, icebound wilderness. The ice had closed up quickly behind me, making the pathway invisible, except for the wonders of technology.

Earlier explorers didn't have that luxury. If they found themselves in my situation, on a day when the sun was obscured by fog, they'd have had to do it by dead reckoning – working out on the compass where they'd gone and what distance they'd travelled and then trying to draw it onto the map. But, this far north, they couldn't even have done that. Compasses don't work up here, their direction confused by the closeness of the magnetic North Pole. So those earlier adventurers would have to guess their pathway out of the ice and it would be very, very easy to get stuck again. Many of them did get stuck, and many of them died.

It was about 10 in the morning before I was sure I was clear. I sat in the cockpit and watched the sails lifting. I've never been so happy to hear the sound of water rushing under the bow.

Everything was the same – the fog still sank the edges of the landscape in grey; the water still lapped over pieces of floating ice, turning it mottled and dark. The seals still lounged on their ice ledge. It made no difference to this place whether I was trapped or free, but I'd had my wake-up call.

I grabbed a beer and it went straight down. I might even have had a second. *Astral Express* was clear.

I knew now that I needed to avoid this ice field. I'd sail further east, give it a wide berth and come back in to the west. That's what I did, sailing in clear water, and after another day's sailing Lancaster Sound was up ahead.

Eighteen thousand miles I had sailed to get here, solo in my yacht, since setting out from Auckland, New Zealand, almost at the opposite point on the globe. Now before me lay one of the great enigmas of sea exploration – the Northwest Passage, filled with mystery and adventure, and probably more stories of loss and failure than triumph. In the early days many died trying to discover it. Many who attempt this passage even nowadays get into difficulties either with poor equipment, or the wrong type of vessel, lack of preparation or seamanship, or – as in my first attempt – adverse weather.

There are no records of anyone having sailed the Northwest Passage solo and unassisted, as I was about to do. Even sailing it non-stop would be a first. But, as I made my approach, this so-called record had no bearing on my ambition to attempt it. This was a personal thing. A challenge, a dream, an adventure. This was what the trip was all about, and here I was at the entrance.

1

A PROPER CIRCUMNAVIGATION

"Above all, we had been around the world, and there is magic in those words."

—Eric Hiscock, *Beyond the West Horizon*

"I'm thinking of sailing around the world." I was sitting by the fire with my family in our holiday home at the Marlborough Sounds one rainy Easter holiday. Daydreaming, staring into the flames, my mind loose – isn't this how people since the dawn of time have begun their adventures?

"Non-stop," I added, following up quickly with "Solo."

There was a bit of a pause. I waited for the negative reaction. It didn't come. No-one said I was mad. No-one said I couldn't do it. Maybe they thought if they didn't say too much the idea would just go away.

I had almost surprised myself. Saying it was thinking out loud, and this was the first time I'd really thought about it. But once I'd said it, it was like an idea that was right – it had a logic and a rightness, as if everything I'd done up till then was leading in that direction. We pulled the atlas out and started pouring over it, figuring out the best way to go. That's where it kicked off, and after that the idea grew.

I wanted to sail solo around the world non-stop, leaving from Auckland and returning to Auckland. Sailing from the Southern Hemisphere via the Northwest Passage around the world is not an easy thing to do solo and non-stop. It's never been done before. Some people sail up to the Atlantic, get close to the United Kingdom, do a U-turn and then sail down again, but I didn't want to go up one way and come back the same way again.

Most circumnavigations are done from the Northern Hemisphere, for instance from the United Kingdom or France. They take a southerly course down the Atlantic, skirt around the Southern Hemisphere below Australia, New Zealand and South America, and return again sailing back up the Atlantic.

I didn't want to just go up and down the Atlantic. As we poured over the atlas I could see there was another way of doing it, by incorporating the Northwest Passage – the temperamental, unreliable waterway that links the Atlantic and Pacific oceans above Canada and Alaska in the Arctic Circle. With that in the mix, it all seemed to gel. I'd always been intrigued by the idea of sailing through the Northwest Passage. I don't like cold weather, and the Antarctic has never attracted me – but I've always had a hankering for the Northwest Passage. I wanted to sail in the wake of heroes.

Over the next year or two I did a lot of research. I came to the conclusion that wind and currents through the Northwest Passage were generally more favourable if travelling from east to west. I also saw that by taking the east–west route I could judge both earlier and more accurately if it would be open enough for small-yacht navigation. Coming in from the east side, it's easier to make an exit if it proves not to be open. Coming from the west, however, you must sail about 600 miles over the top of Alaska before you can be sure of navigating through the Canadian part of the Northwest Passage. If the Alaskan part is clear of ice it is usually straight-line sailing. But the Canadian section meanders through and around headlands and islands in a vast, icy maze. If it turns out not to be clear enough to get through, you can get iced in trying to retreat.

The east-to-west approach also suited the course from New Zealand. I could sail the Tasman, navigate north of Australia and then take advantage of the east-to-west trade winds across the Indian Ocean. Okay so far, but it presented the daunting prospect of sailing the Cape of Good Hope from east to west. I would have to be at the entrance to the Northwest Passage by the end of August as it's passable only for about the first three weeks of September each year. This meant I would need to leave Auckland in April, and I'd be rounding the Cape of Good Hope – that famously stormy convergence of wind and current at the southernmost tip of Africa – during the winter. However, if I could achieve that safely, I'd be on course to sail north up the full length of the Atlantic, up between Canada and Greenland, through the Northwest Passage, around Alaska, turning south through the Bering Sea. Then south down through the entire length of the Pacific, where I'd also have east-tending trade winds, and back to Auckland. Phew.

I stared at the map. It would be 28,000 miles. Seven months of solo sailing. No port calls. Could I do it?

I quietly mentioned the idea to close friends. To my surprise although there was no negative reaction, there was also no surprise reaction. It was as though if I said it then they expected I would do it.

I think I've been pretty brave in most things I've done in life – business, life in general. You might say I like a challenge, but I see it more as being open to opportunity. A challenge is something that might be too hard – but if a door opens for an opportunity it's not so much a challenge as just something that makes me feel optimistic and excited. I am an optimistic person. If something feels right I'll be optimistic about it. I see the glass as half full rather than half empty, without being reckless.

I would be nearly 60 when I set off. But sailing around the world wasn't a late attempt to make something of my life. Not at all. I'd already made something of my life. I didn't have to do it to complete my life. I did it for the adventure.

By that stage I'd done a lot of sailing – a lot of cruising, some ocean racing. I'd done a couple of yacht deliveries and realised that people were quite impressed with my delivery and sailing skills. It occurred to me that I'd done my apprenticeship and this thing – this circumnavigation – wouldn't be out of the question.

It seemed the right time. I was in the second half of my 50s, financially secure enough to contemplate the cost this trip would incur, and I wanted to do it while I was still fit and strong. I didn't doubt myself, whereas maybe 15 or 20 years earlier I might not have had the same feeling that my experience was enough to do this. It's not to say someone couldn't do it at a younger age, but maybe doing it without my depth of experience they would also need a bit of luck. And I didn't want to push the luck. I wanted to rely on experience and planning.

If I let this opportunity slip by, I had a feeling that as I got older and reached the stage where I no longer had the physical ability to do it then I would have a regret. *I should have done that when I had the capability.*

I thought it would be good to sign off with having done a solo around the world, and this would be about as complete a circumnavigation as you could get. My route covered 28,000 miles. The world is 24,000 miles round. I'd be sailing 32 oceans and seaways. It was what I'd call a proper circumnavigation.

I was always prepared to drop this crazy idea if anything about it proved unworkable. I'm a great believer in the idea that if a door shuts, or too many doors shut, then you forget it. Life sends you in certain directions. Some things work out, some things don't.

But if an idea is any good it will flow, and this one just kept flowing.

2

AN EARLY TASTE
FOR THE WATER

Ah! what pleasant visions haunt me
As I gaze upon the sea!
All the old romantic legends,
All my dreams, come back to me.

Sails of silk and ropes of sandal,
Such as gleam in ancient lore;
And the singing of the sailors,
And the answer from the shore!

Till my soul is full of longing
For the secret of the sea,
And the heart of the great ocean
Sends a thrilling pulse through me.
—Henry Wadsworth Longfellow, "The Secret of the Sea"

Cruising. To be out on the ocean, travelling from one place to another. No timetable. Just enjoying the journey, stopping when you get there or when you find a place that appeals. Dropping anchor in a deserted bay. Being the first to create a footprint on a beach in paradise.

There's no road out there. There's no highway. You can go where you like. You can choose the country you want to go to – the port or the island or the bay. It's perfect freedom.

These things have fascinated me since I was very young. At primary school we read *Treasure Island* and, like generations of kids, I was absolutely intrigued by all that – the islands, the schooners, the treasure marked on a map. There was a TV programme in the early 1960s called *Adventures in Paradise*, which featured a handsome sea captain called Adam Troy who sailed the Pacific looking for adventure. It was easy to get excited by stories of the sea, and those ideas of adventure have always had their hooks in me. As I grew older I read every sailing book in the library – the early explorers such as Sir Walter Raleigh, Sir Francis Drake, Magellan, James Cook and more recent adventurers such as Joshua Slocum, Bernard Moitessier, Thor Heyerdahl, Eric Hiscock.

I had an early taste for the water, although my first experiences were not in the ocean but in the meandering Heathcote River, which curled through the suburb of Beckenham where I grew up in the South Island city of Christchurch. My earliest boat memory is that when I was four a small wooden rowing boat appeared in the backyard of my parents' house in Southampton Street. What I didn't notice at that age was that my father had built it. The first use I put it to was to fill it with water and make a pool to cool off in with my friends during our hot summers. You could call it reverse boating, with the water on the inside.

My next foray came several years later when I built a canoe. I went to the local cycle shop and collected several spokeless wheels, which I hacksawed in half to make frames for the canoe. I used wooden stringers, canvas and old house paint, and I was soon navigating the Heathcote River.

It was only towards the end of my years at Cashmere High School that I began to sail dinghies on Lyttelton Harbour with friends on summer days. But however much I enjoyed the sailing, I distinctly remember thinking how much nicer it would be on a larger yacht that didn't capsize.

After leaving school at 18 I worked around the clock, saving money for a ship's ticket to the United Kingdom, and in July 1965 I set sail on the *Northern Star* ocean liner. It was my first time properly out on the ocean, and it gave me a taste for it, and a love of the Pacific and its many islands. I decided it was from the deck of a yacht that I wanted to get to know this part of the world.

I was away for two years, but as soon as I returned I promptly began building a 35-foot trimaran, beginning with floats or outriggers. Looking back, the logic seems silly, but I wanted to be sure that by the time I came to build the main hull I would be a more experienced builder. The design was by Hartley, and plans and construction were quite easy. I got the outrigger and main frames for the hull finished when romance and marriage intervened. Luckily I sold the floats to someone who had built his main hull first. I had no regrets and enjoyed the family life that followed.

My advice to friends has always been to charter a boat or yacht, and not to own it. I never took my own advice, and I was just 24 when I bought my first yacht.

This was the *Galatea*, a 32-foot kauri classic built by Tom le Huquet in Auckland in 1910. I travelled to Nelson, stayed with a friend and on a fine Sunday morning went aboard this huge vessel with its pleasant owners. We enjoyed a calm day on Nelson Bay with the sails hardly filling. We had lunch and tea and I thought: *This is paradise.* I promptly bought the yacht. That's how little things can change your life. Had it been a stormy day – sails flapping, water coming in, too rough for lunch – there's no way I would have bought it. How many people are put off by their first introduction to sailing?

I joined the Lyttelton-based Banks Peninsula Cruising Club, and was a member right up until I moved to Auckland shortly before setting out for the Northwest Passage. We sailed *Galatea* locally, racing and cruising, and a few times up to the Marlborough Sounds, 200 miles by sea to the north of Christchurch.

Galatea was the start of my offshore sailing experience, and many yachts followed over the years. Cars and boats – I loved them both, and raced them both at various times. I had some business success young, and by the age of 25 I also owned the *Aderyn Mor*, a Thomas Colvin-designed 42-foot steel ketch. This was the platform for a boys' trip to Fiji where we were joined by wives and girlfriends who flew there to get their first taste of the tropics in the Pacific.

Cruising has been my first love in sailing, and in my next yacht, the 50-foot Alan Mummery steel-sloop *Astral Rose*, we headed for the Pacific – Hawaii, Fiji and especially Tahiti. Tahiti is a dream for many Europeans, whereas for us it's right next door. French Polynesia is probably my favourite cruising area – there's some feeling there, something that draws me to it. It's some magic combination of climate, geography, the mix of French and Polynesian cultures, the coral, the reefs, the atolls. Moorea, Bora Bora, Huahine, Raiatea – I can understand how the mutiny on the *Bounty* came about, how those pale-faced English sailors from their harsh backgrounds were drawn to the freedom and the warmth.

We sailed probably 100,000 miles in *Astral Rose*, cruising or racing her every weekend and holidays. We became boat people, and a lot of our friends were boat people, too.

Racing was an interest, but never really a priority. I did it mainly because it honed my skills for cruising. Racing teaches you how to sail properly. How to set sails. How to maximise. Also, if something's going to break, it will break when you're racing because you're putting so much extra demand on it. If your boat is strong enough to race, it will last forever when you're cruising.

In the 1980s I bought a racing yacht called *Pastime* – 45-foot, built in 1886, purported to be the oldest sailing boat in the world still sailing under its original rig. A real classic. I bought it because there had been talk of it leaving the province and I felt that for historical reasons it was important it stay. I had it for three or four years and we did a couple of gentle races in it, and sailed it a few times. I gave it an anniversary celebration at the yacht club in 1986. It's a beautiful boat, now looked after by a trust which is restoring it.

Pastime had been raced competitively for huge prize money, back in the day – up to 35 pounds a race. That doesn't sound much to us, but when you realise that you could get to Australia for three pounds, or furnish an entire house for 35 pounds, you see that it was a considerable amount. Because of the money to be won, boat owners then as now would make adaptations to their boats to make them go faster, and *Pastime*, which was owned by a boatbuilder, had been lengthened to increase its speed.

Nothing's new. In fact in boat design I realised that the 19th-century *Pastime* still had the same principles for racing as the monohulls have today – the way a boat is ballasted with lead, the way the rigging is put on little shelves to get the angle bigger, the use of a bowsprit to get more sail area, the gaff rig which all the new boats have (that is, they've got batons at the top of the sail to give it more area). Some of the older racing boats even had internal ballast they could slide from one side to the other – every key principle of those boats is in boats today. The difference is in technology. The keel shapes are different, the hull is built of lighter materials, as are the masts.

In the early 1980s I was involved with a syndicate that had a Formula 40 racing catamaran, which is the forerunner of the type of America's Cup boats being sailed now. We used to sail it up in Auckland and it was fast – one day we hit 34 knots.

Around the same time I sailed in the Kenwood Cup, run by the Royal

Hawaiian Ocean Racing Club, because I had a friend who was skippering the boat.

I was invited to do a promotional leg on *Lion New Zealand* with Peter Blake and Grant Dalton in the weeks after they'd won the 1984 Sydney to Hobart race, sailing as a guest from Bluff up to Lyttelton.

In 1986 I sailed in the Whitbread Round the World Race with Digby Taylor aboard *NZI Enterprise*. We were in the lead on the leg from Auckland on our way to Cape Horn, racing hard, when a fitting broke up the top of the mast and down she came. We had to go back to the Chatham Islands and arrange to have the boat taken back to the mainland. I took it up from Lyttelton to Auckland, motoring all the way. It was a shame – Cape Horn is the only major cape I haven't sailed around.

Then in 1987 my friend Stan Pearson and I sailed *Astral Rose* in the inaugural two-handed Melbourne-to-Osaka race. That was a real ocean experience – 5500 nautical miles, an epic journey that crosses multiple weather systems and seasons across the Pacific Ocean. That was another of those perhaps crazy ideas that turned out to have legs, it worked out. We were in a cruising boat rather than a racing boat but nevertheless we tried to be competitive. Although we did very well, in hindsight if we had really wanted to be competitive we would have needed to have a cutting-edge racing boat. That was quite a big exercise, getting *Astral Rose* to Melbourne, then to Osaka. From there, Stan took it to Honolulu and left it for nine months and we took a family holiday on it up there.

I sold *Astral Rose* in the 1990s and Tahiti beckoned with the purchase of a waterfront house in Moorea. But that was a fleeting dream. Although I would like to have lived there permanently, I was outvoted.

All the time I was gaining more experience, getting further away from my early experiences of struggling with the day's sailing on *Galatea*.

Keeping up my interest in sailing, I also did various delivery trips. So, overall, I had a lot of experience in different types of boats.

Having time to sail was always balanced with being able to make enough money to live a modest lifestyle and educate four children. I've been self-employed since the age of 25, with a business career that culminated in farming and residential property. Getting started, I understood how to operate in the economy of the 1970s with its rampant inflation, and through a series of stepping stones managed to put together a lifestyle that I enjoyed with my family – on a 400-hectare farm within the Christchurch City area that I bought in 1985, aboard our yachts, or at our holiday home in the Marlborough Sounds.

Eventually my business success was what enabled me to undertake my around-the-world trip on *Astral Express*.

It is interesting that many people with money don't have time. Money should buy you time – it's no use having one without the other. Money is always there to be made, time isn't. Money should give freedom, not be an obsession. Make a little and spend a little, that's my philosophy.

In my late 20s I took a break from business. My wife wanted to pursue her career, so I stayed home and looked after the children – getting them off to crèche or school, making lunches, being there when they got home at the end of the day. I was a house-husband before it was common. It was fun. I went to Canterbury University and did some philosophy papers. I'd made money young, so I chose to use it on a lifestyle I very much enjoyed at that time. I used it to buy time for things I thought important.

There's a quote from the mountaineer George Mallory that sums up my feelings about this: "What we get from this adventure is just sheer joy. And joy is, after all, the end of life. We do not live to eat and make money. We eat and make money to be able to live. That is what life means and what life is for."

It would be a shame to face our Maker and find out that we'd done it all wrong. When you consider our predicament on this ball floating in space, it doesn't pay to take it all too seriously. As long as you're considerate of others, it's best to do the things in life that make you happy.

3

WANDERLUST

The fair breeze blew, the white foam flew,
The furrow followed free;
We were the first that ever burst
Into that silent sea.
—Samuel Coleridge, "The Rime of the Ancient Mariner"

There I was at age 12 – a skinny kid, short back and sides, shorts, T-shirt. I'd been brought into our local radio station, 3ZB in Christchurch, it must have been for children's hour. The studio light came on, and I was on air – Graeme Kendall, reading two verses of Samuel Coleridge's "The Rime of the Ancient Mariner".

Perhaps the idea of sailing around the world had always been there, waiting for me.

There's not much left to explore in the world. Much as I admire James

Cook for his skill and his ability to navigate and to accurately record where he had been, it's the times he was living in that I envy. Everything was still wide open for exploration and discovery.

As a sailor I had that same wanderlust, that longing for the freedom to explore. But everything's been explored – there are no new islands. We know where everything is. Even the Northwest Passage, the elusive, serpentine seaway across the top of Canada and Alaska connecting the Atlantic and the Pacific oceans, is there on the map now.

My hero Captain Cook had been among those who searched in vain for the passage. In 1778 he led an expedition of two ships, the *Resolution* and the *Discovery*, up to the Arctic Circle but got only as far as Icy Cape in Alaska before they had to turn back, only narrowly escaping the gathering ice.

In 1845, two ships led by John Franklin, the *Erebus* and the *Terror*, carrying 129 men, became trapped in the icy vice and simply disappeared. One of the ships was finally discovered on the floor of the ocean in 2014. Many other ships have either disappeared or been "crushed like a nut on the shoals and buried in the ice", as Canadian captain Henry Larsen, the second man to sail the passage west to east, said.

It was Norwegian polar explorer Roald Amundsen who first navigated it by sea, over three years in 1903–06, during two of which he was entirely iced in.

So, like everyone else now, I knew where it was. I could trace it with a finger on the map. Yet it tantalised me. It hadn't been sailed very often. Sailing the Northwest Passage presented itself to me as an opportunity to do something that had not often been done before. In fact, as far as I knew no-one else had sailed it alone, or over just a single season.

Satellite technology and warmer Arctic conditions have contributed to making this milestone achievable, but the challenge is still immense. I knew I risked becoming stuck in the ice, but in most years there is a window of opportunity when the ice melts enough to make passage possible, if one has a boat that can sail fast enough.

4

THE PERFECT BOAT

The boat was designed and built to do that particular job. Reliability and endurance were paramount. You couldn't have any breakdowns. It had to be durable enough to withstand all the weather over a long period. Graeme's circumnavigation was a very long distance, especially for one person. It was a great achievement. It demanded a partnership between boat and sailor. The mental attitude and the equipment had to be of the same standard.

—Greg Elliott, boat designer

Victory awaits him who has everything in order – luck we call it. Defeat is definitely due for him who has neglected to take the necessary precautions – bad luck we call it.

—Roald Amundsen

Finding the right boat to carry me around the world was the first and most important step. I wanted a fast, strong yacht with inside surveillance. The ideal scenario, in terms of both timing and cost, would have been to buy an existing yacht that I could modify for the venture, but nothing suitable was available.

So I began looking at options for a new boat and soon settled on the Greg Elliott-designed Tourer. This is a fast cruising yacht with level cockpit and main saloon with windows at eye level. With the help of Auckland yacht broker Terry Needham, I visited several yards where yachts of this design were constructed. It seemed perfect for what I wanted.

The Tourer design comes in lengths from 12.5 metres to 15.5 metres and, in line with my philosophy that the smallest boat able to do the job is the best one, I chose the 12.5-metre version, especially after discussion with Greg Elliott. I did a test sail on one from Sydney up to Brisbane with boatbuilder Peter Newman who, as well as being a seasoned sailor and racer, was a partner in the Melbourne boatbuilding company Blue Marine. I decided the boat was ideal, and I put in an order which included some modifications.

This model was produced from moulds in Melbourne by Blue Marine. Peter was instrumental in overseeing construction that produced the perfect hull and interior for my needs.

Hi-Modulus in Auckland designed the hull lay-up and provided the Kevlar necessary for strength and impact resistance in the Arctic. Kevlar was laminated into the mould and an extra 8-mm section of it was wrapped around the bow. It was this strong hull and bow that would protect me from being crushed in the ice, or holed by submerged ice. It was bulletproof. I was keen to see just how strong it was, and took a piece of laminate home to the farm in Christchurch. I gave it a full hit with a long-handled axe and fired two .22 bullets at it. The gel coat chipped under the axe, but nothing penetrated the Kevlar.

The boat's shell – the hull, decks and engine mount – was shipped to Auckland aboard *Tauranga Chief* in December 2004 and transported to the America's Cup building in the Viaduct Harbour for its fit-out.

I found the right boatbuilder to project-manage the remaining stage of work. Philip Wilson had had his own boatbuilding business for many years but was now a marine consultant. He is a professional in all aspects of boatbuilding and its associated requirements, and finding him was key to the success of what I was about to do.

Philip employed two boatbuilders and the three of them plus myself put the rest of the boat together over the next two months – all the electronics, engine, mast, rigging, wiring and so on.

I was always researching products and design, and Philip would listen to my ideas and subtly suggest changes if he didn't agree. Together, we produced the perfect boat.

———

Nothing was left to chance. If on a trip like this something happens that you don't expect, then you haven't done your homework properly.

Over the years since I'd first begun to grow the idea of sailing around the world, and especially in the two years leading up to the boat's construction, I did endless research. Every single item of design was carefully considered and chosen for a reason – for weight, for strength, for function, for quality. I thought very carefully about everything that would be needed. I never hesitated to seek the advice and opinion of other people. I chose sailmakers, mast builders, engine and electronics suppliers and then took their advice, always in consultation with Philip Wilson and yacht designer Greg Elliott. I always requested: "If you think any part of my preparation is not correct, say so."

It was an excellent working relationship.

At that time I had the finances to buy the best product, so I didn't have to make choices based on economy. I could simply choose what I thought best.

Cruising yachts can be quite luxurious – big double bed, fancy upholstery. There was none of that in *Astral Express*. It was all as basic as we could get it, minimalist you might say. This boat was being built for a particular purpose, and so all our thinking was channelled into that purpose.

I had responsibilities to family and friends. This was not a suicide mission and I didn't want to rely on other people for a rescue.

I didn't want to get out there on the ocean and after a few days think, "I'm not happy with this." And I never ever felt that. I never felt I was in the wrong boat. As it turned out, I was happy with all the decisions we made.

There was no doubt it was an ambitious project. The boat had to hang together for 28,000 miles, and be safe through the ice. It had to be self-sufficient – an enclosed system – able to carry not only all the supplies I'd need for the non-stop journey, but to generate its own power for the communications and electronic technology. Although I was planning to sail, I needed to carry fuel for emergencies and also to power the generator. I needed to carry water, but also the means to restock water supplies. It had to carry absolutely everything that I'd need, and nothing else.

I eliminated anything that could jeopardise my success. If it could break down I didn't want it on board – consequently I didn't have a fridge or a water maker. Anything that might break but which I absolutely needed, I'd have two of: two steering systems, two autopilots, a spare rudder, a spare way of getting water to the engine if it iced up or blocked, phones, radios, satellite navigation, water supply.

Meticulous attention to detail is paramount in this kind of exercise. It's the same in anything – car racing, racing a yacht or flying an airplane. You need the right people to put the right things together to make it safe and efficient. It really matters.

Luckily, I could use the internet for research. Twenty years earlier it wouldn't have been so easy. I had every item searched; I knew exactly the weight of everything I was putting into the boat.

Weight was the crucial matter. I needed to carry a few tonnes of gear – everything needed for body and boat over 28,000 miles and six months – yet every kilo on the boat is a kilo you have to push through in the water and the wind. It adds to the time of the journey. Over 28,000 miles any extra weight takes its toll. Often it's a cost matter – it costs more to make a light boat because the materials are better quality.

By the time it arrived in Auckland from the Melbourne boatyard, the boat was finished, structurally. However, one issue had to be sorted out and that was that the windows around the boat's cabin were too big for New Zealand's category 1 offshore requirements. Unless we could tick all the boxes we would not get clearance to leave New Zealand waters. Something needed to be done.

Also, although they were as solid as anything, we were concerned that the edges of the windows were vulnerable to being knocked by fittings. So we built a fibreglass surround that fitted over all those windows and that solved the problem – although it cost a further $40,000 for that one item.

After discussion with people who had crewed on vessels through the Northwest Passage, I knew I needed a lifting keel and retractable mounted rudder so I could navigate close-in if ice-free channels opened near the shore, or if I got stuck in ice and needed to float off. The Tourer model comes with a lift keel as a standard feature, one of the reasons I selected this particular boat. It was hydraulically operated by an electric pump, and it could also be hand-pumped even higher. In this way the boat's keel depth could be altered from 2.7 metres to 1.5 metres.

We changed the original design slightly to ensure the propeller and the sail drive were fully protected by the back edge of the keel. Even with the keel right up, the sail drive sat just above it. It was as safe as you could ever get it from being damaged in the ice.

Most boats the size of *Astral Express* have a rudder underneath, but we put the rudder on the back of the boat – like a dinghy's rudder across the back, dropping down through a case so it could be lifted up and down. Usually that sort of rudder has a tiller, but of course I was going to be using autopilot and the only way to get the autopilot big enough to work was off a wheel-steering system. So we had to figure out how to steer the rudder off steering wheels. It took a lot of brain work and sketches and working out the geometry.

Being able to see the action of the rudder was a great help with the autopilot trim.

One problem, especially when sailing alone, is how to safely get up the mast if repairs are needed aloft. To solve this I purchased a rope ladder that could be attached to the mast and hauled up by a rope halyard.

I also had folding steps attached to the side of the mast going up about four metres to the mast spreader. This was a good place to sit and look out when spotting ice and ways through ice.

The whole bow section was blocked off with a bulkhead, which is like a wall with an access door in it, and this for'ard end was filled with polyurethane foam, in blocks, for buoyancy. If I hit an iceberg and holed the boat up for'ard, the boat would stay afloat. Five buoyancy compartments were built in.

The back starboard corner of the boat, which sailors call the quarter berth area, was set up for food storage. I had plastic boxes that all fitted together, stacked neatly in. I got very particular with setting things up, to the extent of having only two knives, two forks, two cups and a couple of small pots.

For sleeping I had two single pipe berths fitted each side of the main saloon. These are aluminium frame bunks, more like hammocks really, and they hinged up and down according to the angle of the boat. I'd sleep on whichever was to the windward side, and could lie flat even when the boat was leaning over.

The area with the toilet and basin was the only interior part finished to a normal boat standard. Quite large and white-lacquered, it was a great sanctuary for a tidy-up. The rest of the interior remained finished in the light tan colour of the composite construction. It was very spartan.

Rather than cabin doors, we had canvas fitted over openings with zips around them, just as you have in a tent. Even the toilet "door" was this style. It both saved weight and also prevented the problem of doors banging in a storm.

It was the same with the storage areas. They were open bins – plywood fronts with a big hole cut in them for access, and canvas covers to close them off so everything didn't go flying around. That's what all racing yachts have.

Because the bow of the boat was full of foam we couldn't put an anchor locker up there, which is where you would normally put it. Instead we stowed the anchor winch, chain and rope right beside the mast. That was good from a weight-distribution point of view and, of course, I didn't plan to stop and anchor anyway.

I had to carry enough food for six months. Apart from catching fish, I could not supplement my diet in any way. For this I took the advice and help of nutritionist Jeni Pearce, who was also dietician to Team New Zealand. She designed a balanced diet consisting largely of freeze-dried food, and then prepared it into weekly packs – 28 in all. They were numbered and carefully stowed on board in order.

———

During this busy time people would ask me, "What have you been up to?"

"I'm planning a trip around the world," I'd reply.

"Oh, great," they'd say. Then: "What else are you doing?"

"What else?" There was nothing else.

ENABLED BY TECHNOLOGY

But then one night the short wave suddenly broke through, and [our]
call signal was heard by a chance radio amateur in Los Angeles who
was sitting fiddling with his transmitter . . . It was a strange thought
for us that evening that a total stranger . . . was the only person in the
world but ourselves who knew where we were and that we were well.
—Thor Heyerdahl, Kon Tiki: Across the Pacific by Raft

Thor Heyerdahl's great adventure across the Pacific on a raft of ancient
design took place in 1947, and at the outset he had been reluctant to
consider relatively newfangled shortwave radio. It wasn't what the
explorers of old would have had, after all. Yet he came to realise the great
benefits of being able to send messages home. In fact, he and his fellow

sailors sent a 75th birthday message to the King of Sweden and received a reply from the King himself.

Such are the wonders of technology.

One of the keys to Captain Cook's success was that he also made use of cutting-edge technology – in his day the sextant and the chronometer. Put together with his other skills, this equipment enabled him to know where he was, explore and map it methodically, and find it again. They were key to his discoveries and his cartographic achievements.

In the same way, new technologies enabled me to sail solo around the world. I had GPS (Global Positioning from Satellite), ice charts, satellite communication. Autopilot was essential and I was to use it 99 per cent of the time. It took the place of a crew, in that I could hold a direction without having to physically steer. This technology in no way took away from a sense of achievement in the venture. Rather, it enabled me.

Research was paramount in planning and trying to execute such an ambitious idea, and that's where the internet was invaluable. I am sure this was the defining factor and advantage that I had over earlier explorers. Having that technology and being able to access it on board to gather weather and ice information was what enabled me to contemplate sailing around the world solo without being irresponsible. Knowing exactly where I was at any given time, knowing my speed, knowing the current wind forecast, made the trip more scientific and less risky. To sail the Northwest Passage with modern electronics and satellite surveillance would give me the edge that few other Arctic explorers ever had. I would know the course to take and hopefully the conditions ahead, whereas earlier explorers had to consider a myriad of options to find their way through and around the headlands and islands of northern Canada. Do I take this course? Do I pass this island left or right? No wonder that in this hostile environment many got lost and perished.

I installed alarms to alert me to shallow water, or – when I was sleeping – if the boat had moved off course, or the wind changed more than 10 or 15 degrees. Of course, if the alarm went off I'd wake up. But in reality by the time you've spent much time on a boat you're so attuned to the feel of the wind and the water that you wake up with the slightest change anyway.

I installed an electronic tracker so my daily progress could be followed by those onshore.

The autopilot, the navigational instruments, the music I'd have playing, the LED navigational lights – all these things were going to chew through the power. So power supply was integral to the success of the venture and to my independence as a solo sailor. But for all the technology on board none of it is intuitive – there is only one brain on the boat.

I carried 750 litres of diesel fuel. The engine was 40 hp, but apart from a dire emergency it was only for charging the batteries. We mounted a large alternator on top of the engine so I could charge the batteries quickly. But we needed alternative ways of charging the batteries. We installed flexible solar panels all over the cabin top, and a wind generator on the back of the boat.

Sun, wind and diesel – three power-generation systems. I ended up with more power than I needed, which was really good. Sometimes I could go for three to five days without using the engine at all as the solar panels and wind generator kept the batteries adequately charged. The solar generated around 10 amps, which is the size of a moderate-size battery charger if charging your car overnight. But when conditions turned cloudy, cold and calm, the engine was essential for keeping the electronics running.

The fuel was stored in four ballast tanks and Philip designed a transfer system so that I could pump it up to the windward side of the boat to simulate two or three people sitting on the rail to help stability.

The freshwater system was pretty basic. I had a very small water tank, 140 litres, and some bottled water for emergency reserves. But I also collected water and that was often enough. We made a canvas extension to the canopy outside, with a drain in the centre for collecting rainwater. It worked well and I could fill up the water tank with that. Of course the canvas would get dirty and I needed a good ten minutes of rain to clean it out, but after that I could start collecting. It was difficult at times because generally it would rain when it was a bit stormy, so I'd have wind blowing the water away. But a nice tropical downpour with no wind – perfect. It was wonderfully basic.

We did have a pressure water system on the boat which also had a hot-water cylinder heated off the main engine, but I very rarely ran that. I used the hand pump most of the time to save power, and also because when you're hand-pumping you use far less water than you would otherwise. All my cooking was done in seawater – I'd just draw it in by a foot pump.

What would happen if the water inlets bringing seawater into the boat to cool the engine, and also for the galley and toilet, froze up? In response to that risk, we built a big rod that you could push down through the pipe to clear the ice out of it to get the water flowing. That's just an example of the many little things we had to think about as we prepared the boat.

Looking back, there's not much I'd do differently, given what was available at the time. I think I was pretty thorough in my planning. Perhaps, in hindsight, given I wasn't using the engine for propulsion, I could have had a smaller, lighter engine which in turn would have used less fuel, meaning the boat could have been lighter overall.

Of course, since then technology has continued to improve. If I was to do the trip now I might install a go-pro camera system. Being solo, I couldn't really do any filming. If something was interesting I was far too busy to film it. And, of course, battery systems for storing solar and wind power are improving dramatically all the time. But I don't think there's much I could have done differently at the time.

By the second leg of the trip, five years later, I was able to install a better, faster and cheaper computer system that enabled me to download my own weather information and ice charts more often, thus making me more independent. But in the beginning, I was more reliant on people back on land for up-to-date weather information. In particular, Roger "Clouds" Baddam from Team New Zealand was vital.

For that first stage, Dave Schnackenberg from Personal IT took charge of my blog and he did a very good job, helping me with computers and downloading photos. For the second leg, my son Joel came into the picture more and was instrumental in doing the blog for that part and helping with the weather. I had great moral support from him during difficult times.

6

CLEAN BILL
OF HEALTH

At first I simply didn't believe him. It wasn't until I actually stepped aboard the boat myself that I thought – he's serious! I knew some of the seas were the worst in the world. I thought it was severely dangerous to be by himself in such a small boat. You can't guarantee that someone will survive. But at the same time I was very excited. My dad's sailing around the world. How many people in this world can say that?
—Jessie Kendall

Preparation was key not only for the course and the boat, but also for me. At 59 I had done my apprenticeship regarding sailing experience, but I had to make sure I was mentally and physically fit for the task ahead.

I made several visits to the doctor and dentist and got a clean bill of health, for the next six months anyway. I was concerned about staying awake at crucial times and thought medication might be required for this, but was advised coffee would be just as good.

Of course, I carried a full medical kit for emergency use. Broken bones and severe cuts were the most likely things to prepare for, and, of course, a good supply of painkillers was essential. If you can numb the pain, you can get on and deal with the injury. I knew I could make an international call to my doctor for medical assistance and detailed instructions if necessary.

Sailing regularly and doing weights at home kept me toned, but it was doing yoga at least once a week that was a key element in my preparation. Flexibility and balance are magic attributes on a small yacht at sea.

In warm-down at the end of my yoga sessions, I would visualise as many aspects of the trip that I could, so that later when it came time for the real thing I sometimes felt that I had done it before.

After the trip was all over, when I'd returned home after completing the Northwest Passage, making it back through the Bering Sea and then the Pacific single-handed, people often expressed amazement that I'd done all that "at that age". I think my age was compensated for by my fitness preparation, and also by my experience. But like most people, I just don't feel any different, inside myself, to how I felt when I was thirty. My father lived till 93 and right up until his late 80s he said, "I feel really good but I look in the mirror and I see an old man."

So 60 might seem old to some people, but it really isn't old. An 85-year-old might say, "Toughen up. At 60 you *should* be able to do it."

It would be easier if we didn't know how old we were. Imagine that: if all we had to go on was how we felt inside ourselves. I'm absolutely sure that knowing our age, we limit ourselves according to the expectations of others. Because we know our age we think we should act a certain way.

By 60 many people are bored with their career and want to retire from it – but the word "retire" shouldn't be in our vocabulary. They retire from their career and they retire from life. They put themselves out to pasture, and that's the danger. The best thing you can do as you get older is get a new career. At least get a goal. Get something to inspire you.

Our bodies change and we do grow older. You can't fight that, or be unrealistic. We are not teenagers any more, and nor would we want to be. But we are *able* – to be honest, I was surprised at just how able I was. And we have all that experience to draw on.

Use it or lose it. Everything in moderation with the emphasis on both words.

Have a good diet, watch your weight and generally keep fit all the way through. Yoga is great, and the older you are the more benefit you get from it.

None of this is rocket science.

If the Rolling Stones can do what they're doing at 70, why can't I sail around the world at 60?

―――――――

At last, on 23 February 2005, *Astral Express's* sails were put on, and on 26 February launch day arrived. Gently she was lowered into the water down at Auckland's Viaduct Basin as a large crowd looked on. She was floated to her water lines and a party followed with speeches, advice and congratulations.

Through March and April I trialled her out on the Hauraki Gulf. I raced her a couple of times, then sailed out to Great Barrier Island on my own, did a circumnavigation and stayed aboard a couple of nights. I didn't get any bad weather, but I felt very comfortable with her. I think my project manager thought I hadn't tested the boat hard enough. But I was confident. The homework had all been done two years before.

The whole exercise was enormously expensive – over double the price of a normal boat at that time. It was obvious that I should consider finding a sponsor to offset the cost, but various factors put me off that idea.

The first was that it was difficult to find a sponsor who truly understood what I was trying to do. After discussing the plan with several companies I soon realised that my plan to sail around the world non-stop via the Northwest Passage was too ambitious for them to conceive. I may as well have said I was off to the moon. They didn't think it was possible and, of course, no-one wants to back failure.

Added to this was my determination to rely on my own judgement at all times. I had always said – and meant – that if at any stage something didn't feel right, I would abandon the project. This would not be possible with a sponsor on board, and I didn't want that pressure.

So I decided to pay for everything myself – after all, that's what most boat owners do with their pleasure boats – and immediately felt relieved. Then I turned the problem around. I would become a sponsor myself. I realised I could use my journey to raise money for a children's charity I cared about, and so I formed a relationship with Variety: The Children's Charity and carried their logo, along with a phone number which automatically generated a $25 donation. It was a good partnership, as Variety is international and is based in several of the countries I passed along my route. As I passed each country I contacted their head office by phone to inform them of my sailing attempt so they could use it for their benefit, and I later found out that as I sailed past, donations were made to the local Variety chapters from interested followers.

The checklist seemed never ending, but as April approached things had to move quickly. The ideal departure date was late that month as I needed to have traversed the 18,000 miles to Lancaster Sound, the entrance to the Northwest Passage, by late August. It was a carefully calculated timeframe. As I said earlier, the Northwest Passage has an approximate two-to-four-week window of navigation if the summer ice melt is sufficient. Leaving New Zealand in April, all I could do was calculate and hope that Arctic conditions would be favourable by August and September.

Early signs looked promising for 2005.

All I had to do was get there.

7

SAILING AWAY

The ship is bought and fitted. She lies at anchor, ready for sea . . .
—Robert Louis Stevenson, *Treasure Island*

A small crowd of around 100 family and friends gathered on the dock in Auckland's Viaduct Harbour that Tuesday morning in April 2005.

I'd been up early making a final check of the provisions, of the boat and all the equipment. My children did a last-minute supermarket visit. My eldest son Nathan bought me a full box of fresh apples. That was great as apples are really the only fruit you can keep on a boat – they last until they run out. I enjoyed these ones for the first six weeks at sea. I was given gifts – coffee, wine, blankets, fruitcake and books.

My nephew Gareth Ramage, who helped put the boat together in Auckland, gave me a Fedex box. "If you go crazy out there you can talk to Wilson," he said, a reference to the Tom Hanks movie *Castaway*. I tucked the box inside the boat, but I never did open it.

Now was the hour. Would my family ever see me again? I felt confident and calm. If my planning and preparation was as good as I thought then they could feel confident, too. My eldest daughter Rebecca commented that while I was saying goodbye it was clear I was already a step ahead of everyone else – I was already on my journey. It was probably true. After the years of preparation, I was more than ready for this adventure to begin.

I cleared Customs, and then *Astral Express* slowly motored out of the Viaduct Basin and set sail to circumnavigate the globe with this silly old sailor doing it alone.

We all know what it's like – you're not on holiday until that aircraft door closes. When that door closes you know there's nothing more that can possibly be done. You can't change your mind about what you've packed. You've got your passport, you haven't missed the flight. It's done.

Cruising's the same. It's all in the preparation. Usually the preparation time for a boat trip is as long as the trip itself. In my case although there had been two years of planning, once the "go" button was pushed *Astral Express* was about six to nine months in the making, which was about the length of the trip.

Once you head out into the harbour, what's done is done. The journey begins.

What have I forgotten? But there was nothing I'd forgotten. As I sailed away from my crowd of well-wishers, I ran it all through in my mind, but there was nothing.

I sailed out past the Auckland landscape; past the familiar cone of Rangitoto Island, the extinct volcano about 800 years old just off the coast of the city's northern bays; past the beautiful headlands and small islands, heading north and leaving my homeland astern. I waved to friends who'd driven around the shore to vantage points to see me sail out.

Being a week day there were not many boats about, just the occasional sailing boat and the usual ferries moving up and down the coast. Auckland is very spread out and people commute long distances to work in the city. Weekends, however, are a different story as these waters are a fisherman's paradise, with boats everywhere enjoying the many sheltered bays in the cruising grounds of the Hauraki Gulf.

It did feel strange to be leaving home – my home in this isolated South Pacific paradise. I felt it in my chest – my pride in being part of this country that regularly punches above its weight in so many areas. Most people know about the All Blacks and Edmund Hillary – but do they also know about Ernest Rutherford being first to split the atom? Or that we were first in the world to give women the vote? We are pioneers in so many ways. As I headed out into my own ultimate adventure, I was already telling myself that every mile I sailed was a mile closer to getting back home again.

For the first few hours I sailed mostly calm and sheltered waters. A kind southwest wind at 15 knots carried me up the coast towards the Bay of Islands, and the day passed quickly as I worked to set the boat up properly and arrange everything below, stowing away the last-minute supplies and gifts. I didn't have much time to dwell on the trepidation of departure, of leaving family and friends behind, or the coming arduous adventure.

Later that day I noted in the log book a message to myself:

"Courage, discipline, experience, faith. Think it through. Caution. To sum up: vigilance and diligence."

———

But by nightfall the wind had gone around to the northwest and by midnight just north of Whangarei it was really howling. It was around 55 knots and because it had come up so fast the seas grew very steep.

Normally a boat of this type would have one large sail up front. I had chosen to have two smaller ones – a cutter rig. They were both on roller furlers that rolled the sail up like a blind by pulling on a line attached to a drum at the base of the sail. This line led to the cockpit at the back of the boat, so sails could be safely controlled from there. The larger mainsail, attached to the mast, was also able to be reduced in size by hauling on two lines controlled from the cockpit. So sail reduction could be made quickly and efficiently without having to go forward on the deck.

Of course, when it was necessary to go up front, or to work at the mast, my harness could be clipped on to a continuous safety line attached to the full length of the deck on both sides. One of these was also placed in the cockpit. Rule No 1 to Rule No 10: don't fall overboard!

I got my wet-weather gear on and quickly reduced sail. The wind was quite quickly harsh. Gosh, I thought, I've set it up so I can reduce sail, but can I reduce it enough? I reefed the mainsail down, rolled the headsail away, rolled out the staysail. I had it reduced as small as I could get it, but even like that it was very vulnerable to the wind.

In such short seas the boat was being slammed by violent waves then crashing into troughs, the front of the boat smashing on the water underneath and stopping suddenly. She felt strong, but if she was going to break, it would be in these conditions, the mast succumbing to such shuddering battering. The wire side stays were attached to the deck by carbon fibre. So far they were drum tight.

It was a hell of a test. Throughout the trip I was to have many breezes stiffer than this, but that first combination of wind strength and the direction and shortness of the sea made it very challenging.

We describe a sea as "short" when the waves are very sharp and close together. For instance, when I was in the Bering Sea coming south past Alaska, the storms were fierce and relentless but they blew for days. So the waves, while they could be 12 metres high, were as much as 100–200 metres apart. In those kinds of conditions, if you're lying a-hull with no sails up or you're running with it, you're really floating over them and down. But when the sea's short it lifts the boat high and sudden, and then drops you into the trough.

And, of course, I was tacking into it, which was making it worse – if you're running with it, it halves the effect. There were some outlying islands I was aware of and trying to avoid, but once I got past them I could lay off a little and adjust the course.

By the time dawn broke the wind was easing. Everything was in good shape. The rigging was still drum tight. Mother Nature had dealt an early test. If *Astral Express* had been going to break, this was a good time for it to happen. I could have limped to shore and fixed it, or canned the whole thing. But she'd come through intact. I was tired but happy.

As the light grew, I faced northwest. It wasn't long before I passed North Cape at the tip of New Zealand and headed out into the Tasman Sea. Land disappeared behind me, and in front of me stretched the world's oceans.

8

NORTHWARDS, AND FIRST LANDFALL

The soul of a journey is liberty, perfect liberty, to think, feel, do just as one pleases. We go on a journey chiefly to be free of all the impediments and of all the inconveniences: to leave ourselves behind, much more than to get rid of others.

—William Hazlitt

My plan was to sail north through the Coral Sea, into the Great Barrier Reef and around Cape York, the northernmost point of Australia, then enter the Indian Ocean and catch the trade winds to the Cape of Good Hope, South Africa.

But first, the Tasman, which stretches from the bottom of New Zealand to not quite the top of Australia. Some sailors fear the Tasman and, it's true, many boats and lives have been lost in this stretch of water. There can be cyclones, or just the regular southerly fronts that storm up from the Roaring Forties, meeting the warm, southbound Australian current sweeping down from the tropics. That meeting can be explosive and terrifying.

I was lucky. After that first storm I enjoyed easy weather. Norfolk Island was my first landfall, around 800 miles from New Zealand's North Cape, and I reached it on the fifth day after leaving Auckland, sailing happily with a 6–8-knot ESE tailwind in fine conditions.

I saw it at dawn, escorted by a school of 20 or 30 dolphins who I felt were welcoming me to the land. I sailed around the island, close enough to see houses and buildings and trees, and I called up on the radio to say hi and tell them what I was doing. But it wasn't long before the island slipped behind me and once again the ocean was all I could see.

My daily routine was starting to set in. At this stage I could usually sleep at night, albeit in short bursts. I had alarms set to warn me of nearby shipping and wind shifts. I set the autopilot to steer so I was free to navigate and to trim and set sails to keep *Astral Express* moving as efficiently as possible. With the autopilots doing their job I had time for all my domestic duties as well – cooking, cleaning, repairs, exercise and communication. The mornings went fast but by lunchtime, after writing the log with the day's position, the afternoon dragged. I'd usually read. The best thing was my iPod, loaded with over 5000 songs, and I had it playing most of the time.

I looked forward to happy hour at 5pm. Then after my rum and coke it would be time to cook the evening meal.

I had the fishing line out and was starting to feel good. There's nothing like a fishing line to make you realise you're on holiday. I quickly realised it was no use having the line out at night because unless I was monitoring it constantly anything would be eaten by something other than myself. But on the other hand, fish were caught more often at dusk than dawn, and that was often a bit late for my evening meal, which was usually over by about 6pm.

But apart from such a minor quibble, all was going very well. I was heading north up to the Coral Sea, and the weather was growing warmer day by day.

―――――

I'd calculated that I needed to do 150 nautical miles a day in order to be at the entrance to the Northwest Passage at the end of August.

A nautical mile is 1.15 miles, or 1852 metres. That distance is figured out by getting the circumference of the earth at its widest point – around the equator – and dividing that circle into 360 degrees. Then each one of those degrees is divided into 60 "minutes". Each one of those "minutes" is a nautical mile. A nautical mile is longer than a land-based mile because the nautical mile accounts for the earth's curvature, whereas the mile does not.

Sailors measure speed in knots, and one knot will take you one nautical mile in one hour.

In that early part of the trip my whole focus was on keeping my speed up. The wind was generally light, so I always needed to concentrate on sailing the boat to its best ability. In fact I averaged 150 miles a day, which is about six and a quarter knots, and that turned out to be ideal.

Astral Express was a thoroughbred-designed boat, and no matter how light the wind she could sail at least 100 miles a day. I was happy to have chosen a boat with such capability, and I knew she could have done 200 miles a day if I had a crew and really wanted to push it. But by maintaining 150 a day I was being realistic, and that calculation had determined my leaving date. If I'd left any later I wouldn't have been able to get up to the Arctic at the right time. When I did get up there around four months later, the people who live up there and who I was talking to by radio were amazed that I'd left New Zealand in April to be there on time. But I'd designed everything so carefully, and that in itself was an achievement.

I would be sailing through oceans I had never sailed before.

The world's oceans are really, of course, one continuous, interconnected body of water. Yet people have divided them up and named them with reference to the continental landmasses they abut. There are five oceans – the Southern Ocean, Indian, Atlantic, Arctic and Pacific. The bottom of South Africa, for instance, delineates the Indian Ocean from the Southern Ocean, but if you come down the Indian Ocean and keep sailing, it's not as if you'll notice anything different. There is no line or sudden shift of conditions.

These oceans are interspersed with smaller bodies of water – seas and gulfs. I was to sail all of the world's oceans and 23 seas. I was about to get a lesson in the true size of this planet of ours.

———

Two weeks out of Auckland I'd covered 2000 miles, caught my first fish, an albacore, and successfully tested my rainwater collection system.

The sunsets at that time of year in early May were around 6pm, and they were spectacular, the perfect happy-hour entertainment. Perhaps there were tropical thunderheads on the horizon – at any rate they looked like atomic explosions, night after night.

I had begun to notice that I always had a bird flying around the boat, not the same one but always one there for company. I began to count on seeing one there, as if it was my guardian angel. However, one afternoon around about 4pm a small bird perched on the lifelines. It was a very small swift – a little, brown bird, perhaps 10cm in size. I thought it was cute and figured it needed a rest. We were a long way from land, at least 500 miles in any direction. It wasn't long before that first one was joined by a partner, and by nightfall I had around 20 of them sitting on the boat. To my surprise, they flew into the cabin and began perching in pairs, on my coffee cup, on the stove, on the pots and shelves and on the rack above my bunk.

I was amazed. I had never heard of this happening before. These birds were obviously tired. I took some photos and then, in the company of my new feathered friends, I too settled down for the night.

It was hot and so I was laid out on my bunk with no covering except my shorts. Of course, when I woke up in the morning there was birdshit all over my leg. I looked around and they had crapped everywhere – on the cups and pots, and especially on the floor. Oh jeez. I shooed them out into the early daylight. They still seemed exhausted. Some of them staggered, and a few had died, but most of them flew away, continuing on their mysterious journey. It was strange and rather wonderful to have this little glimpse into those great migrations that you hear about. Swifts can fly up to six months without taking a break. Godwits fly every year from Alaska to New Zealand. I wondered whether these birds had somehow got blown off their course, which would explain their exhaustion.

I had put myself into their environment, and so I could see the patterns going on around me.

It took about a week before I'd managed to completely clean up after them. The floor was very difficult. It was non-skid rubber with a rough texture, so it needed to be scrubbed several times. This was just around the time when the world was going crazy worrying about Bird Flu, and here I was sleeping with a flock of them.

Some years later, on the island of Vis off the Croatian coast, I was astonished to see some birds that I thought identical to my friends from the Coral Sea. On reflection, it seems unlikely – perhaps the Croatian ones were pallid swifts, but they certainly looked the same, and I find it incredible that birds traverse the planet to such an extent. They are the true wanderers of the hemispheres.

Raine Island sits on the outer edge of the Great Barrier Reef about 620 kilometres north of Cairns and marks the entrance to the Pollard Channel, one of the few channels that allow boats inside the Great Barrier Reef. It's treacherous, and more than 30 shipwrecks attest that intense care is needed. But the only other option this far north was to go even further north and through a whole series of islands that could be quite tricky. It seemed a better plan to get inside the Great Barrier Reef, because once you're in it's quite a large waterway and I could sail up around the northernmost tip of Australia and into Torres Strait and across.

Raine Island itself is beautiful, a low-lying coral cay that has the largest green sea turtle nesting area in the world. It's totally protected from public access. However, my approach was at 1am and it was totally dark. I could see nothing, although the island's stone beacon, built in 1844 and the oldest European structure in tropical Australia, showed up on my radar, which was helpful. You can generally assume the GPS is accurate to within 30 or 40 metres, but in a narrow channel you want more certainty, and the radar signal confirmed the GPS satellite electronic position showing on my chart. I sailed slowly past the island and into the entrance of the channel.

Pollard Channel is only between one-quarter to half a mile wide. I had to be on full alert, paying close attention to the GPS, the radar and my depth sounder. I was lucky. The breeze was light and warm, and when daylight came I could see the Australian mainland – the massive, low-lying, barren hinterland – and the open waters inside the Great Barrier Reef.

The Great Barrier Reef lagoon is a good five or six miles wide all the way up that North Australian coast. I looked back the way I'd come. The water just stretched calmly, with nothing to indicate the treacherous dangers beneath. In the old days, without the GPS and radar, there was no way any sailor would attempt that channel at night. Even in the daytime you'd only approach it if you had a really good chart, and if the weather was calm. If I'd had rough weather I would have had to lay off till morning, but I was always reluctant to pause. I was always conscious of my timetable and the need to keep pushing on.

This channel was the first big navigational challenge of my around the world trip and I was very relieved to have made it through. I was also tired after my all-nighter, and it was hot – 32.5 degrees in the shade. A few charter boats worked their way up the shore, but otherwise there wasn't much traffic. So I set the autopilot to sail north, set my alarms and lay down to catch a little sleep.

Next day I did some calculations. My daily average so far was 140 miles per day. I'd need to increase that to an average 157 nautical miles per day if I wanted to get to Lancaster Sound in time. I had to keep pushing. I'd been having light winds, so I needed to maximise the wind I was getting. I used the multi-purpose spinnaker whenever possible. This is housed in a sock that squeezes the MPS inside it so that it's ready for use whenever it's needed. The sock is simply hoisted to the top of the mast so the spinnakers can fly. No pole is required, making it ideal for single-handed sailing. To take it down the sock is pulled down and the sail lowered on the deck. It was all very easy in these light conditions, although a solo sailor is like a one-armed-paper-hanger when it's blowing hard. Being bright orange, the MPS could be used as a marker in an emergency.

———

Torres Strait links the Coral Sea with the Arafura Sea in the west, and is the narrow waterway between Cape York Peninsula, the northernmost tip of Australia, and Papua New Guinea. It's one of the busiest shipping lanes in the world with thousands of vessels passing through each year, but it is actually extremely hazardous. Not only is it shallow but it is a veritable maze of 580 coral reefs, more than 270 islands and shifting submarine sand dunes.

Great, and again I was approaching in the dark. I reached the entrance to the strait around midnight. If the weather had been rough I would have waited till morning but, as it had been at Raine Island, the weather was clear and calm, so on I went. I sailed close to the southern side to avoid the deeper waters where most of the large ships navigate in depths of only 13 to 20 metres. I had my eyes wide open looking for ships, and I had my radar to help me also. Fortunately, it wasn't very busy that evening and during the night I saw lights from only about 10 vessels. The ships that come through there are often huge things, 50,000-tonne container ships, so I was pleased to have struck it while quiet.

Being night, I couldn't get much impression of the land, although of course I was hyper-aware of it from my charts and radar. On my starboard side I could see nothing, but quite some way through the strait I saw a town on my port side – I could see the lights on the buildings as I slipped through unnoticed.

Things started to get tough about three in the morning. I was tired, much more so than I'd been coming into Raine Island where I'd had a pretty quiet day beforehand. This time I'd been navigating hard as I approached Torres Strait, so I was probably a bit tired already when I reached the entrance. So by three in the morning I was pushing it, but I had to stay awake for at least another half hour to clear the strait.

I made strong coffee and took five-minute standing rests against the back of the helm chair inside. It's surprisingly restful and without the risk of nodding off if you were to actually lie down. I would never lie down unless I had everything set up with alarms. But in this case, standing and leaning on my helm chair gave me the little burst I needed. By 4am, with dawn just breaking, I had two islands ahead at about

30 miles and beyond those the open waters of the Gulf of Carpentaria. I desperately needed some sleep so I set the boat on course with alarmed way points before these islands, and put my head down for about two hours' sleep. That worked fine, and as often happens I woke up about five minutes before the alarm sounded. Sometimes when there was a ship coming on the radar, I'd wake up five minutes before the alarm would go off – probably coincidence, but that's what would happen.

I made more strong coffee, and sailed past Warral and Ului Islands, out of Torres and into the open waters, on course to sail north of Darwin and then west-south-west towards the Indian Ocean.

The Gulf of Carpentaria is the habitat of saltwater crocodiles – another good reason, I noted to myself, not to fall overboard.

It was 32 degrees and the wind was light. I felt a tug on my line and pulled up a fish. Everything was going well.

I was careful to sail closer to the Australian coast than to Indonesia, as pirates could be a problem in this area. As I entered the Timor Sea just past Darwin, I was alerted by a call on the VHF radio – a woman's voice asking me to identify myself. She was speaking from a light aircraft flying overhead that turned out to be Australian Customs doing their regular surveillance of this area. They asked my port of departure and destination.

"Are you ready for this?" I responded. "It's Auckland and Auckland." I suggested they look up my website. Happy with this, they flew off and I could hear them later asking other ships in the area for their details. Over the next three or four days the plane made several appearances, each time flicking its wings as it flew over, asking if everything was okay and wishing me a pleasant trip. I knew they were more interested in stopping refugee boats coming down from Indonesia than pirates, but it was comforting to know I had company in this sometimes dangerous area.

9

THE INDIAN OCEAN WAS VAST BEFORE ME

We were in the path of the real trade wind, and every day would carry us farther and farther out to sea. The only thing to do was to go ahead under full sail . . . There was only one possible course, to sail before the wind with our bow toward the sunset.
—Thor Heyerdahl, *Kon Tiki: Across the Pacific by Raft*

The plan had always been to take one day, one week, one headland at a time and watch the miles as they peeled off the back in my wake: each mile made was one less to cover. It was a mental attitude that kept me focused and grounded. Otherwise the thought of those huge distances ahead of me could have been daunting.

As I came down over the top of Australia, heading south to catch the best currents and the trade winds, the Indian Ocean was vast before me. It was about 6000 nautical miles to my next landfall at the Cape of Good Hope, South Africa, a journey that would take around six weeks, with a further six weeks from there up to the Arctic.

The trade winds would blow me across the Indian Ocean. That time of year – by now it was late May – was pretty well perfect for catching them. That was one of the reasons I went north around Australia rather than south. Going south was the shorter distance, but you risk the sou'west and westerly gales. Going around the top was longer but easier going, and then you have the benefit of the trade winds.

Everything about my course was designed so that I caught the best winds possible. I'd looked at the world's weather patterns, the currents, the winds, and designed my route accordingly. The trade winds generally blow from east to west, so that was the way I went. Going that way meant a couple of unavoidable challenges. Going east to west around the Cape of Good Hope was famously difficult, and coming down through the Bering Sea was also well known for adverse conditions. But everything else about the course should be favourable.

As I entered the Indian Ocean, everything was going according to plan.

By this stage I had a good daily routine. With the Indian Ocean before me I really felt that things were settling in. Body, mind and boat were all in good shape.

As I pointed out earlier, my nutritionist had prepared weekly food packs, one to be opened each week. Because my first day of the journey had been a Tuesday, each Tuesday now became opening day – a bit like

Christmas Day. What would be inside? I'd dive into the good stuff – there were always treats like lollies, chewing gum and chocolate. Less desirable stuff like muesli bars I'd put in my grab bag for emergency food, just in case I ever had to jump off the boat in a hurry. It also contained a spare phone and water.

My main meals were freeze-dried and they were great, with several curries, lamb and beef dishes and vegetables. By this stage of the trip my fishing tackle was working well, and I regularly had fresh fish to supplement my supplies – mainly small tuna, such as skipjack, albacore and yellowfin.

While I had never taken food supplements in the past, I decided they would be a good idea in these circumstances, just in case there was any nutritional deficiency. So I took Omega 3s and multivitamins daily.

I structured my days around normal patterns – night-time sleeping, daytime awake.

There were times in the middle of the ocean when I could sleep for six or eight hours if I needed to, and sometimes I did. I'd be miles from anywhere, well away from any shipping lanes. I'd put my radar alarm on, then I might go to sleep from say 8pm till 10.30, get up for an hour or two, and then go back to sleep until six in the morning. Those times were great – I'd be up with the sun, having a coffee, and live the day like I would at home.

I've been asked if I got worried, going off to sleep like this when there were possible obstacles in the water such as containers or logs. My reply is that you have to be a bit philosophical. If it's going to happen, it's going to happen. But I've never seen a container under water. I've never seen anything in the water in all my travels that was dangerous to run into. Maybe I've seen a log of wood in the harbour. The chances are that even if I did hit anything submerged, depending on the angle it would glance off. And *Astral Express* was strong enough to hit ice, so I wasn't too worried. Are there containers floating around? Containers are heavy – you'd think they would sink to the bottom.

Even if I'd had a very disturbed night – due to bad weather, for instance – I'd be up at daybreak. I knew that if I'd only managed two or three hours sleep I could catch up with catnaps during the day. But I always stuck to my morning routine: get up, make coffee, eat muesli, check the course, check the boat, do some cleaning. I'd exercise in the cockpit, practise as much yoga as I could manage in that confined space, and do some squats to keep my legs active. It's the legs that deteriorate on a boat. Your shoulders and arms are working but you're not walking anywhere. It's important to pay attention to overall fitness.

So the mornings were busy and went well. I'd sometimes have a call to make, and then it would be time to think about lunch, which I'd have around midday. Then I'd write up my log book – distance, mileage, conditions and so on.

The afternoons could be a bit slow. In hindsight I would have taken more books – the ones I had I read thoroughly. Nowadays, of course, I would have a Kindle and even be able to watch movies. But it's fair to say that those hours between two and five could drag sometimes. I think it was boredom rather than loneliness that got its hooks into me. If there was a storm, the hours flew by.

But then, if the weather was good, 5 o'clock would roll around – happy hour. Rum is the traditional sailor's drink, and it makes good company for a chat to oneself. So I'd pour a rum and coke (everything in moderation), sit in the cockpit and take the time to reflect on the distance I'd covered that day. *That's 150 miles less I have to do.*

Sometimes, in truth, I would grow a little pensive and philosophical. In my logbook after a particularly philosophical session, I wrote: "I am not a poet, unlike some, but it's surprising what comes out of a glass of rum." I made that time each day to remind myself that I was feeling good, that the day was an achievement, everything was working well and I was enjoying myself. What could I do better? What had gone wrong? What was good and what could be a problem? It helped the day go by and was very good psychologically.

I don't drink much now – less and less, actually – but back on shore I'd usually have a glass of wine with dinner. So I guess doing it on the boat was bringing some of that day-to-day structure into the life of the boat.

The structure of the day is very important on a boat, and the schedule I'd created worked well for me. I was feeling good, sleeping well, exercising. I felt enthusiastic about whatever was going to happen. Happy hour was just another part of that day. Five o'clock. A time to sit down and assess. Then at 6pm I'd get busy again, make my dinner, then move on to the routines of the night.

Loneliness wasn't an issue. Of course I thought of my family and friends a lot, but I knew I was going to see them again soon, and I had very good communication on the boat. People could call me up. *Where the hell are you?* Or I'd call someone. That was the thing that most set me apart from earlier sailors. When Captain Cook set off on a journey he waved goodbye and simply wasn't heard of again for years.

I don't think I would have contemplated it without that communication, partly for my own benefit but also because it would be so hard on the people you've left behind if they didn't know where you were, whether you were alive or dead.

I liken *Astral Express* to a self-contained office. I had a telephone and a computer, I had information on where I was and where I was going. I had a unit on the boat that sent my position out twice a day so people at home could get on their computer and see where I was. I had music playing all the time and that was a form of company. So I really didn't feel isolated.

Certain changes take place when you're on your own for a while. Your thinking changes. You take a different perspective on things. I had time to really listen to the music. Lyrics and songs are much more poignant when you're on your own. Sometimes I'd get emotional, thinking about this person or that person. Not in a bad way, in a good way. I still felt very connected to people. I also knew it wasn't forever. I'm a social person. I didn't want to be a solo sailor all my life. I just wanted to do this particular thing, and I was enjoying it. It was a new experience.

At night I sat out in the cockpit and stared up at the stars. Our own galaxy would take 100,000 years to travel across at the speed of light. It would take 93 billion light years to travel across the diameter of the observable universe. I tried to comprehend it all – the billions of stars and billions of galaxies. Some physicists even postulate that there are multiple universes. I twisted my mind trying to think about it all, and then I thought: there's no point. It's infinity. Better to go back to thinking about the things I can actually see. A sunrise. The beauty of the sky. For me the miracle of life and the driving force of self-replication – of producing children who would live way past the end of our own lives – seemed a stranger, more miraculous phenomenon than the universe itself.

I was outside at every opportunity. Unless I was cooking, sleeping or navigating – or if it was just too wet – I much preferred to be out in the fresh air. I'd bring my meals out to the cockpit and eat with my plate on my lap. I was always keeping an eye on things – on the boat, on the world around me, on the weather.

I watched the clouds, which are like art in the sky, and I tirelessly watched the birds. The more I watched, the more intrigued I became. They were a huge part of my journey, a constant presence. The only time in the whole trip when there were no birds to be seen – in the last section of the Northwest Passage in the grim Beaufort Sea – I felt spooked, as if there was something wrong with a place that not even the birds wanted to be in.

For hours I watched them as they cruised the air. I noticed how infrequently they dived. I watched small birds flittering like wind-up toys, white terns with their slow, deep wingbeats, and heavy albatrosses lumbering along, scarcely moving their wings. I watched birds gliding down and then finding the lift of the wind off the waves. They'd flick their wings for power and glide up and down. I felt a real kinship – me in my sailboat, experiencing exactly the same forces as them, of wind and current. Sailing is vertical, flying is horizontal, but we were both riding the wind. Needless to say, they were far better at it than me.

There were stronger trade winds to the south, so I headed that way, needing to increase my speed. All the time I was trying to make the boat go faster. If I was going six knots I'd be trying to get seven. If I was going five knots I'd try and get six. I trimmed the sails properly, and I went looking for the good winds. If a weather forecast said it was better in the south, I went south.

I used the MPS, the spinnaker, although using that in anything but light weather is not totally safe. At the beginning you're working on the front of the boat. The sail fills quite vigorously, and then if you've got to get it down quickly later if the wind changes or it gets too strong, that can be an issue. If I was going to fall over the side it would be when I was handling something on the foredeck, so I really only used the spinnaker on this first part of the trip, up to the Arctic, when speed was a necessity. Coming home I used it a couple of times, but the second time I got in a bit of a tangle and thought, what's the point?

Of course, I was very careful about safety. I mentioned earlier that the deck had a safety line on both sides all the way from cockpit to the bow. I wore a harness with an inflatable jacket and a line I hooked on to the boat's safety line, so when I walked to the front I always attached myself. But I could still have tripped and fallen and had to pull myself back on board. And, of course, if I was to hurt myself and get a hit on the head as I went over, there was no-one else to help. So I was very alert to the dangers and safety. But using that spinnaker in that part of the trip wasn't so bad because the winds were light.

My average speed was 6.5 knots to 8.5 knots, although sometimes I would surge to faster speeds. To get that average I had to be in those higher speeds for four hours. My best day's run was 196 nautical miles. To hit 200 miles would have been very good progress indeed – it's like hitting a century in cricket.

It would have been easy to do more than 200 if I had had crew. Because it was just me I was on autopilot, which isn't always as efficient as someone steering. The autopilot takes you in the set direction regardless of the wind, and the wind could shift four or five degrees, and I probably wouldn't shift the steering or trim the sail. I guess you could say the autopilot is better than one crew member but not better than three or four, because if you had three or four crew one would steer the boat as they saw the sea, and the other would be trimming the sails to get the best out of the wind, or changing the sails where necessary.

It's also obviously easier to do a high mileage day if you're going in a favourable direction, but if you want to keep on a particular course, as I did, you have to take what you can get.

———

On 1 June the weather changed and some rain squalls came in, so I managed to catch a few litres of water. With the wind now southeast I was on a steady westerly course to Madagascar. It was fresh and bumpy at night and I sailed with two reefs in the mainsail and storm jib upfront. The solar panels and wind generator kept the batteries full. Because I'd sailed a little south the temperature had cooled to 28 degrees.

On 7 June I passed a quarter of the way around the world. I had Mauritius Island at 600 miles and Madagascar at 950. Cape of Good Hope was 2300, about 14 days away.

I stared around me. What a huge ocean this was. There was definitely no shortage of water in the world, I mused. Just take the salt out of it. A fraction of the current global military expenditure would solve this with desalination plants. I guess it's all a matter of priority.

Day after day, the sun beat down. We wonder at the stars at night, but really only one star matters for us and that's the one that accompanies us through our days. The sun. She runs the show – wind, rain, snow, ice, our seasons, even our orbit through space. She gives energy to the plants that provide our oxygen. She provides light. Nothing is more important to life on Earth than this immense body, its diameter three times the distance between Earth and the moon. She has her own variation of climate change, and it's always in flux. Life on Earth relies on it and has to adapt to its variations, as our climate change is in tandem. When the sun sneezes, the Earth catches cold. By harnessing the energy of the sun we can start to alleviate the carbon dioxide issue as well. But day by day we must respect her, and I was very aware of that as I sat for day after day in the full glint and glare of the sun on the ocean. It's a fine line between getting enough vitamin D and suffering from melanoma from our nuclear reactor in the sky.

I carried plenty of sunblock cream but preferred not to use it all the time – I'm sure that one day it will be found to be carcinogenic. The best plan was simply to keep out of the direct sun as much as possible. I often wore collared T-shirts and unattractive sun hats, and sheltered under the cockpit's spray dodger, especially around noon. Sometimes, here in the tropics, I hung a towel in the cockpit for extra shade from the late sun. It would be a relief to get into the higher altitudes where the weaker sun would be less of a threat.

Meanwhile, the trade winds lightened off and I was now back to sailing every inch of speed I could. I wrote some more poetry: "My boat is small, the ocean is vast. I wish the damn thing would go fast!"

In mid-ocean at about two in the morning I noticed a light on the horizon. I was 2000 miles from any land. I had better be careful out here.

I went inside and got out a parcel I'd been carrying, as yet unopened. I smiled to myself, remembering how I'd gone into a gun shop in Christchurch with my son Joel to enquire how big a bullet could be used in a shotgun. It was midsummer then and so when the guy in the shop asked what I was considering shooting, I just said "Big stuff", thinking if I said polar bears he'd think I was mad. "Probably my size or a bit bigger," I added.

He looked at me sideways.

When we left the shop, Joel asked: "Is it for pirates?"

"No," I said. "Polar bears."

He shook his head. I think that was the moment he realised how serious I was.

Anyway, a parcel duly arrived in Auckland before my departure and now I opened it and took out the sawn-off pistol-handle five-shot shotgun and ammunition. Single-shot lead 12-gauge and five-shot buckshot. It really was intended for fending off polar bears in the Arctic, but now, all alone on the sea, I thought it could also be useful in the event of pirates. I checked the gun, loaded it and sat in the cockpit as the light on the horizon moved closer and in my direction.

After about 20 minutes, a 20,000-tonne freighter sailed past about three miles away and continued on its journey. I was glad it was dark, but I still felt silly sitting there holding the shotgun.

The closer I got to Africa the more of these huge ships, mostly tankers, I was seeing. They can be up to 500 metres long, and very wide too, and they sit low in the water as they plough along doing 20 knots. They come down from Saudi Arabia, too big to go through the Suez Canal, and they go around the southern tip of Africa and then up to Europe or the United States. I've heard that if they get into a big sea and get on a swell they can break their back, but it would take a big sea. Of course, they're constantly weather forecasting, so they know what's around and would avoid that sort of weather.

Three hundred miles from the South African coast, I work out I've averaged 157 miles a day from Torres Strait.

Two hundred miles from the African coast on 22 June and I had my best day's run so far, 196 nautical miles. I caught a lovely mahimahi and did some preventative maintenance as my excitement and my trepidation built for the momentous task ahead: sailing east to west on my own around the Cape of Good Hope.

I was always keeping my eyes open for anything not working properly, and repairing things as they needed it. It was a way of passing the time, but it was also absolutely integral to the success of my adventure. Small failures with equipment inevitably occur, and you have to keep on top of them because a major failure would be the end of the current plan. Dealing with the small failures is the key to success in a mission like this.

This applies to all sorts of attempts where mechanical and electrical design is part of the personal journey – like space travel, motor racing or life itself. You've always got to be fixing things. You have little issues, and the work you put in on little things determines how the big things go. I treat them as issues rather than problems. An issue is something that you get onto and fix. It's only a problem if you can't fix it.

———

At last a long, grey strip disturbed the edge of the horizon, little more than a shadow at first and then solidifying into something tangible. The great African continent.

After such a long journey across the Indian Ocean it was exhilarating to finally see the coast of South Africa. Just to be there. It was afternoon when I sighted land, and by the next morning I was close enough to see, at 30 miles distance, the low, scrubby hills around Durban. A day later, swept by the agreeable current, I reached Port Elizabeth, my intended landfall, passing the headland at too great a distance to see the city but heading west towards Cape Agulhas and the Cape of Good Hope.

With modern GPS you can see the land on your chart and you know you're there and the land's there, and you just think, well, *of course* it is there, the GPS says so. Nevertheless, it was impossible not to feel some of the thrill that the sailors of old must have felt when they found land through their own efforts, by sextant or celestial navigation. It's such a romantic moment in the old stories, and it was a pretty big moment for me. Land ahoy!

10

CAPE OF STORMS

An exceptional wave rose astern . . . I jumped to the floor and gripped the chart table with both arms, my chest flat against it and my legs braced. I distinctly felt the surge of acceleration as Joshua was thrust forward. Then she heeled a little, seemed to brake, and was slammed down hard. Water spurted through the hatch cover joint . . . a huge force seemed to keep her pressed on the water.
—Bernard Moitessier, *The Long Way*

The points on the map that represent the planet's most hazardous challenges – Cape Horn, Cape of Good Hope, Northwest Passage – are hung with the names of the famous sailors who have attempted them. They continue to fascinate us with their dramatic stories of failure and triumph because they really do show Man pitted against the worst fury Nature can throw. On the voyage that was to end with the famous mutiny, Captain William Bligh struggled for a month to get around Cape Horn and in the end had to give up and sail instead for the Cape of Good Hope, which he got around with relative ease, although, he noted in his book *Dangerous Voyage*, the *Bounty* was being pursued by "boisterous weather". He was lucky – countless other ships went to the bottom at the southern tip of Africa, or struggled ineffectually against the seas there.

The thing about voyages and circumnavigations is that the wrong people can get the credit. Take Ferdinand Magellan. He is often credited with the first navigation of the globe, including a passage around the Cape of Good Hope. But while he organised the Spanish expedition to the East Indies from 1519 to 1522 that resulted in the first circumnavigation, he himself was killed barely halfway round, in a skirmish in the Philippines. Juan Sebastian Elcano eventually stepped up to take Magellan's place as captain of the *Victoria*, and it was Elcano who went around the Cape of Good Hope and made it back to Spain.

The sailors of the *Victoria* were much on my mind as I approached the southern Africa coast. They had a terrible time trying to get around the Cape of Good Hope. They were travelling east to west, as I was, having crossed the Indian Ocean, and would have enjoyed the currents that sweep southwards down the coast of Africa. This area is where the Agulhas, one of the strongest currents in the world, runs south down from Madagascar, accelerating westwards around the bottom of Africa to converge at the Cape with the cooler Benguela current that sweeps up from the Antarctic, turning the Agulhas back on itself. Where these currents converge is the "line" between the Indian and Atlantic oceans.

Unfortunately the *Victoria* soon encountered headwinds that became gale-force as they neared the Cape. Not only was their ship leaking, and supplies very low with the crew subsisting on small rations of rice and water, but the storm continued for 22 days, tossing them about and making it impossible to get round. The weather they encountered at the Cape was the worst of their entire trip.

Indeed, the first European to go around the Cape, the Portuguese explorer Bartolomu Dias in 1488, named it Cabo das Tormentas, Cape of Storms – not a bad name.

For all the movement of the currents, it's the wind that causes the trouble. Deadly changes occur when the wind begins to blow from the west and southwest (the opposite direction to the current), and monster waves up to five storeys high are known to occur. There is no way to survive such rogue waves, and even large vessels plunge to the ocean floor without a trace.

Like the *Victoria*, I had come down into the Southern Ocean on a course to pass south of Port Elizabeth. The current was running strong and showed up on my chart plotter screen as a red arrow as thick as my finger, rather than its more usual pencil-thin mark. I figured it must be running at about four to six knots and I was pleased, as it would help me around.

Fair weather prevailed until I got opposite Port Elizabeth, when the wind turned westerly at about 35 knots. A wind of that strength is not normally a problem, but blowing against this strong current coming from the east, it caused the seas to stand on end. It was impossible to sail against. These conditions are what have given this area its reputation as extremely hazardous and the most dangerous cape in the world.

There was nothing for it but to change course and sail into the Bay of St Francis, a huge, scalloped bay, probably about 10 miles long, just a few miles west of Port Elizabeth. I came in really slow and found shelter from the worst of the gale. I was comforted by my decision as many squid-fishing boats were also sheltering in this area. I was close enough to see holiday houses on shore, my first sighting of human civilisation for quite some time. Eventually I lay a-hull in the calmer waters close to land, held almost stationary by the current and wind.

It had been necessary to get out of that wind as those seas could easily have caused damage, but I didn't want to stay long. The weather forecast said the westerly would ease next day, so after less than 12 hours, and with day breaking, I sailed carefully past the fishing boats with their lines out, around Cape St Francis and back out to sea.

I figured that by going out I could have a look and if it really wasn't suitable I could turn around and come back in. What I found was a moderate gale, about 35–40 knots, but easing off to about 20–30. The seas were raging.

But I thought I could do it, and I decided to take the chance.

If the wind was blowing with no current then the longer it blew the longer the waves would be apart, but with the current going against it the distance between the waves stays the same, and as the wind gets higher the waves get steeper until they get so steep that some ships can go right over the top of them, straight down to the bottom.

I probably went out a little bit early, weatherwise, but I could never forget that I was on a tight timetable to get up to the Arctic. However, after six or eight hours of battling, I reassessed. It would be silly to be out there with reduced sail, strong wind, steep seas, boat slamming and not making any progress. I could be out for hours and not move anywhere. The seas were just too steep for me to make my course for the next point, which was Cape Agulhas – the most southern tip of the African continent. Even though it's the official marker of the line between the Indian and Atlantic oceans, it's not as well known as the Cape of Good Hope, probably because it's not as visually spectacular, being just a gradually curving piece of coast with a rocky shore.

So I decided to tack out to sea. This wasn't the straight-line course I wanted – at 30 or 40 degrees off that course I was sailing in an almost southerly direction, only very slightly west, but I was happier doing that than sitting in the bay waiting. When the wind changed I could make a course back. For six hours I tacked out, with the boat still very uncomfortable, water all over the deck and reduced sail, but slowly the wind began to ease off and as it eased off the sea slowly went down.

During the evening a kind 15-knot easterly wind sprang up and with a live easterly and a current as well, suddenly everything was in my favour. I felt blessed and lucky. The storm could have blown for days – it was winter, after all. I would have had to make a choice to sit it out or carry on, and it could have taken me a week trying to make my way around it.

Now about 100 miles from Cape Agulhas, and 200 from Cape of Good Hope, the clouds cleared and I knew it would be a frosty night on shore. Sitting in my cockpit as midnight approached I thought this was the clearest atmosphere I had ever experienced. The air was crystal clear, and the stars seemed to hang so close I could reach out and touch them. They cast a pale light, and in the water the phosphorescence glowed green, peeling away off my bow.

I was feeling good, but it was about to get better. A group of 30 or 40 large dolphins began escorting me, swimming around the boat, some up front but mostly at the back, playing in the wake. It was a pitch-black night and the only reason I could see them was the luminous phosphorescence clinging to their outline. (Walt Disney would have gone crazy.)

I watched for probably two hours and it was an amazing display. They're fast, and as they move through the water they create turbulence in their wake, so all I could see was their outline in green light, then the turbulence. And every now and then they'd break the water and that would make a splash which was lit up with green against the black night. That was one of the best nights of the trip. A night to remember.

The easterly didn't last long and as the wind shifted back to the west, about 20 knots, it was soon kicking the sea up once more. I tacked out to sea again in order to get a good angle to tack back and sail for Cape Agulhas, the true southern tip of Africa. After a few tense hours I made it past by nightfall, past a fairly nondescript landscape, a low, rocky, scrubby shore scattered with wrecks that I could not see but knew were there.

The Cape of Good Hope lay about 60 miles north and I sailed on with slightly eased sheets, passing it around 10 the next morning, five miles to starboard. Its craggy, angular rock faces were a bony finger of land pointing out into the ocean – far more spectacular than Agulhas.

Even though it's not – as people often think – the most southern tip of the African continent, it is still hugely symbolic. It was too early for a rum, but I had a great feeling of achievement to get this far alone and to leave this famous maritime landmark in my wake.

I was also proud to have done it sailing east to west, against the prevailing wind. Of all the parts of the world that I've sailed, that is one that I still think, *Wow, I've done that.* Planning for my trip, it was Torres Strait, the tip of South Africa and, of course, the Northwest Passage that were going to be the biggest challenges, and now I had successfully managed two of them. It would not be my lot to struggle as those unlucky sailors in the *Victoria* had – I had sailed it a full three weeks quicker than they'd been able to.

Over the previous 85 hours I'd had very little sleep – no more than a couple of hours at any one time – but the end of that marathon effort was in sight as I made my way past Cape of Good Hope towards Cape Town. Getting tired is obviously a problem with sailing alone. Here, as in the Torres Strait, I had to stay awake as I made my way north. Boats were showing up everywhere on radar so a close lookout was required, at least until dawn. There were many tankers passing by inshore of me, some looking to be about 500 metres in length, far bigger than the cruise ships that come into Auckland. I could almost measure their length on the radar.

Coffee, soup, chocolate, chewing gum and five-minute catnaps leaning over the back of the helm seat got me through. I wouldn't sleep in it – I never let myself go to sleep unless I had organised all my radars and so on. But those standing naps gave me just enough of a boost to keep me going, and then I was all clear in the morning to head offshore for a couple of hours head down.

The sail north allowed spectacular views of the South African coast between Cape of Good Hope and Cape Town. Being at sea affords magnificent views of the inland mountainous area, the hills and valleys that are so deeply carved they seem glaciated but are simply the result of millions of years of shaping. There are more than 70 peaks above 300 metres within the official city limits of Cape Town, and the Cape Peninsula itself is a mountainous spine jutting 40 kilometres into the Atlantic Ocean.

Happy hour that day coincided with sailing past Cape Town. I could see the windows of the waterfront apartments glinting in the late-afternoon sunlight, and I imagined the people who lived in them coming home from work and sitting out on their balconies, also enjoying a drink at the end of the day. Maybe they'd be looking out at me as I sailed past, five miles out to sea. I raised my glass in their direction.

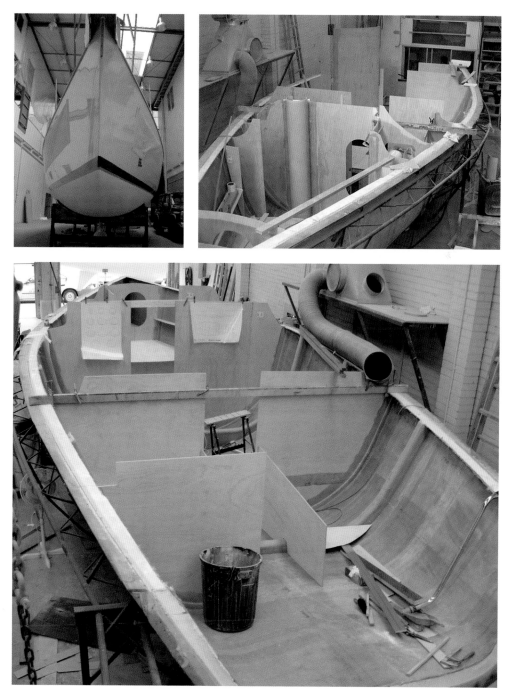

ABOVE: Early stage of construction at Blue Marine's Melbourne boatyard, 2004. Bulkheads and anchor tube being put in place.

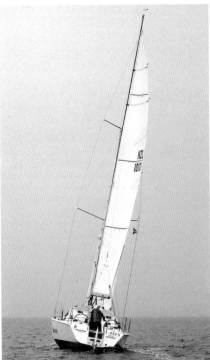

ABOVE: Blue Marine project manager Peter Newman (right) and me.

LEFT AND BELOW: Early trials on Auckland's Waitemata Harbour, 2005.

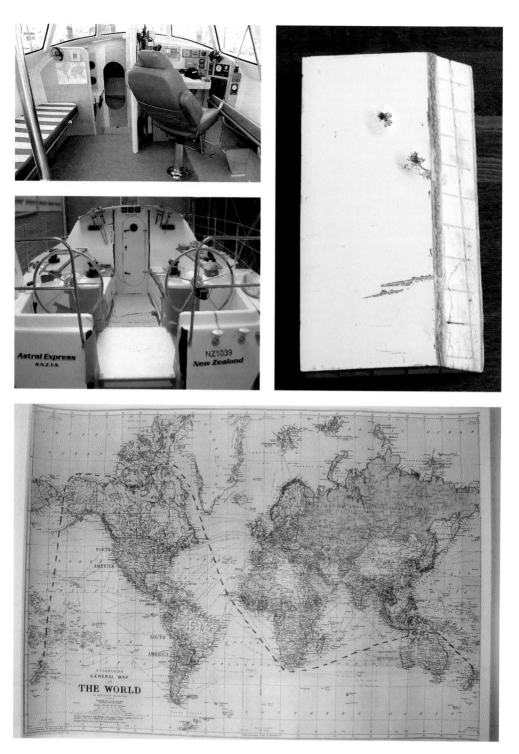

CLOCKWISE FROM TOP LEFT: Sparse but functional interior; Kevlar hull laminate showing bullets and axe mark; The proposed route; Deck hardware was also fitted in Auckland – here you can see winches, compasses, steering aerials, windows, blocks and fittings.

CLOCKWISE FROM LEFT: A typical sunset during the early stages of the trip; Interior of galley and cabin; A day in the office; A typical meal: albacore tuna fried in oil and seasoned with salt and pepper, instant mashed potato and peas on the side; Interior of galley and cabin. Note the weekly food parcel on the floor in its box; and the port bunk where I mostly slept.

ABOVE: Self-invited visitors: the flock of swallows that joined me for a sleepover in the middle of the Coral Sea.

RIGHT: A squall coming in ahead of the boat, bringing rain and increased wind. At night these would show up on radar. They could be intense but they never lasted long.

BELOW: A grand old lady of the mid-Atlantic – close encounter of the turtle kind.

ABOVE: This was my biggest yellowfin tuna. Unfortunately, it was so big I left half for the next day, with dreadful consequences.

RIGHT: Collecting water at night – note the hoses coming down from the dodger.

FACING PAGE TOP: At anchor in Nuuk, in pristine condition. Not even a scratch after four months at sea and 18,000 miles.

FACING PAGE BOTTOM: The Greenland TV crew who joined me as I sailed in to Nuuk. They were my first human contact for over 100 days.

ABOVE: Close inspection: *Astral Express* is lifted by crane out of the water.

BELOW: Edward Niclasen, *Astral Express*'s new owner.

11

GOOD HOPE TO GOOD HOPE

I am a citizen of the most beautiful nation on earth, a nation whose laws are harsh yet simple, a nation that never cheats, which is immense and without borders, where life is lived in the present. In this limitless nation, this nation of wind, light, and peace, there is no other ruler besides the sea.

—Bernard Moitessier, *The Long Way*

If you were to put a line right up the middle of the Atlantic, from Cape Town to Lancaster Sound, that was the course I was trying to take. It took me right out into the middle of the ocean, way out of sight of land.

With some of the toughest sailing safely over, I was on a countdown now for the Arctic, which I reckoned was about 50 days sailing away, my course set northwards into the Atlantic.

Using the Cape of Good Hope as landfall, I would sail right up into the Arctic Ocean, where my next landfall would be Lancaster Sound – almost 9500 nautical miles distant.

I sailed northwards now into the South Atlantic, Van Morrison my favourite choice at the time. *Into the mystic* . . . By the 16th week of my journey, in early July, I was getting back to my daily routine, recovering from the efforts of South Africa, able to sleep again at night with radar alarm on and autopilot steering.

Whereas in the Indian Ocean I'd had to work hard for every mile, the Atlantic was a little more vigorous and my daily runs now were about 165 nautical miles. Southeast winds blew and the Benguela Current pushed north from Cape Town up the western African coast.

Yet again I was struck by the vastness of the ocean. If you fly over it you're asleep or reading a magazine or watching a movie. But when you sail over it, its full scale hits you. There's a lot of water out there – five times as much water as there is land. It puts human life into perspective.

———

A bonus for being so far away from land was that I was out of reach of pirates. I'd been warned about getting too close in to parts of the African coast, especially Angola. I carried a gun to protect myself from polar bears, not pirates. My observation was that if someone's carrying a gun they're likely to get shot. It was very much on my mind that Peter Blake had got himself killed by brandishing a gun. There wasn't much on my boat that pirates would want. No gold. I thought I was safe, but I certainly didn't want to be a hero.

The days went by. Grey skies. Grey seas. I had a page of things to do and was always busy on board. Repair broken sail slides. Assess fuel usage. Lift keel, replace cups at 16 weeks. Check mast seal. Tighten lifeline, tighten steering, check and pump bilges.

Life was simple. My foot-operated saltwater pump was invaluable and made it hands-free at the galley basin. I used saltwater for washing dishes, no detergent, and as long as I washed straight after use it was perfect. I cooked with saltwater and cleaned my teeth with it too. I washed myself daily with baby wipes and took a quick shower each week. I was careful to look after my hygiene and health, and continued to take exercise in the cockpit each morning – squats for my legs and awkward yoga in the confined space on the constantly moving platform.

I mostly slept on the port bunk with feet forward. This allowed me to see the instruments on the chart table and also up through the main saloon windows to the sails and mast. The starboard bunk was hinged up and I used the area to stow books, charts and changes of clothes, all in reach of the leather helm seat which was often a comfortable refuge.

I checked my sail slides and found I needed to replace a couple. They're made of nylon and can break in heavy weather. If two or three were broken and then you had a big blow they could all go and then I'd be in trouble. I'd have to climb the mast and lower the sails by myself in heavy weather, and that was the kind of thing I wanted to avoid at all costs. I was keen to anticipate and avoid anything that would increase my risk of being swept overboard. This was the main danger. The boat was on autopilot, so if I went over the side without being tethered it would be goodbye to the boat. It would just sail over the horizon, leaving me in the water. In that situation, I may as well take a couple of gulps and go under.

I had a remote autopilot control to shut the autopilot down if it was moved any distance from the boat. If I had it in my pocket when I fell in, the autopilot should have turned itself off, and the boat should have rounded up and stopped sailing. I could then try to swim back to it. I never tested this to see if it worked. In fact, I didn't use it much. Half the time I wasn't wearing clothes so I didn't have anywhere to put it!

Most of the time I was clipped into my harness, but I didn't even wear that all the time – although I put it on if I ever took a photo of myself. If it was a really calm day, I just held on as I moved around the boat. I always held on. It's something I do instinctively on a boat, and this boat was designed so there were handles everywhere, indoor and outdoor. A boat can lurch at any time, and greater than the risk of falling over the side is the danger of damaging yourself – breaking a limb or hitting your head.

You have to be mindful at all times. Many have fallen overboard having a pee off the back of a boat. Even with crew on board, people go missing that way. If you were down below and the engine was on, it could be half an hour before you realised someone had gone. So I never did that, especially when I was on my own. All toilet was done down in the appropriate place.

It was slowly getting warmer each day. When the weather gets colder you put more clothes on and as it gets hotter you take more off. If it's really cold you have a lot on, and if it's hot you have nothing on. But I only wore nothing if I was sitting out in the sun relaxing – enjoying the feel of the sunshine, maybe drying off after a shower. Sitting naked in the sun is a bit like having a wash – all that fresh air on your body. So having no clothes on is part of relaxing, and part of hot weather. But more often it'd be a case of not-many-clothes rather than no clothes at all, because if I was working on the boat I wouldn't be naked. For any kind of work I needed my gloves and shoes, and my shorts.

Day-to-day work on a sailing boat is vigorous and often demanding. Properly prepared – and dressed – I could work harder and better with less likelihood of injury. In bare feet you can cut your feet, or stub your toes, or simply not tread as confidently around the boat. Usually the jobs were forward of the cockpit – I'd be at the mast, doing something at the mast or climbing it, and shoes gave me better grip.

With gloves I could hit the job twice as hard as with bare hands. I could handle rope better, and if it slipped I didn't get rope burns. I could grab hold of something even if it was sharp. I could use my hand as a tool – hit something that needed to be hit. And then with my shorts on, I had pockets in which to keep things handy – a knife or a pocketknife, or a handful of screws if I was up the mast.

Inside, the starboard bunk was hinged up, and in that space I had my binoculars, my clothes, my books all handy. That's where I kept my gloves and shoes, and my headlamp, and if I left the cabin at night it was instinctive: shoes on, gloves on, headlamp on, and I was hands-free and ready to do whatever I had to do.

———

Nearly 2000 miles north of Cape Town I passed St Helena Island out east at 120 miles and thought of Napoleon Bonaparte, exiled to this remote place by the British. Perhaps he too spent his days staring out at the sea and marvelling at the size of the planet.

Ascension Island was 400 miles ahead, and my waypoint on the equator, 28 degrees west, was 1200 miles away.

I had relaxed. I was starting to enjoy my own company, laughing at my own jokes, believing in myself. It's inevitable that a boat sailed by a lone sailor is going to become a place where silly ideas swirl, especially the age-old question of the meaning of life. Or should it, I asked myself, be posed more appropriately as the *purpose* of life? The purpose of life is to be message carriers to keep life going, to give others another crack at the apple, but if we don't give it a good crack ourselves then we let down the previous message carriers. That seemed like a pretty neat summing up of biology and the lust for adventure, and I was pleased with myself for my wisdom.

———

Of course, I was checking weather forecasts all the time, happy that reports of ice conditions in the Arctic looked encouraging. The total area of ice in the Arctic has declined in recent years and that year, 2005, looked to have even less, although in the second half of July temperatures averaged below normal over the western Arctic.

There was more ice than normal over the eastern Amundsen Gulf, but there was still time for it to clear, with September being the clearest month for transit. There were enough positive indications to make me hopeful of good conditions, although I knew that wind direction would play a big part as the ice was floating and could move and get congested, preventing navigation in certain areas.

By 21 July I was 3148 miles out from Cape Town, with 4850 miles to go to Lancaster Sound. I had spent three months at sea and at this rate should be at the beginning of the Northwest Passage on time by about 22 August.

It was 33 degrees on board and I would remember these temperatures in a month's time.

12

A BARNACLED OLD LADY OF THE SEA

One could not be lonely in a sea like this.
—Joshua Slocum, *Sailing Alone Around the World*

I was just south of the equator and ghosting along in a zephyr of wind at about two to three knots on a dead flat sea, blueness all around, when something broke the surface just ahead of the boat. It was a Blue Whale, the largest species to have lived on our planet. This one was about 12 metres long, so less than half the size of a full-grown specimen. It was white around its front but the rest of it was a very dark black-blue against the azure of the water.

One minute it was there, then it was gone. It was just gliding slowly on its way, probably doing much the same speed as I was, cutting across my bow. I was going one way and it was going another. I was lucky to see it. For all the sailing I've done I don't see many whales, although I was to sight more as I got closer up to the Arctic.

The whale disappeared, and I got back to what I was doing. It was a glorious afternoon. I was busy on deck, taking advantage of the conditions to cross a few things off my checklist. I was about halfway on my journey so needed to cut and retie all the sheets (the ropes that control the sails) to avoid chafe. I tightened the steering oiled chain on the autopilot, checked the forestay and fixed loose screws on the spinnaker pole, which I carried on board because I'd been advised I needed something like this to use to push off when encountering drift ice.

But every now and then I'd stop what I was doing and scan the horizon, and as I gazed into the blue – blue sea, blue sky – I noticed what looked like a clump of rope floating in the water about 300 metres away.

I got out the binoculars to have a better look and the object appeared to move. So I changed course and sailed over to it. From about 50 metres away I could see it was a huge green sea turtle, about one and a half metres in length. I had no idea how much she weighed but she was big – these turtles can weigh up to 700 pounds, or over 300 kilograms. I came up into the wind and stopped, and we watched each other. It swam towards me, right up to me and we looked at each other. This wasn't like the whale that just went past; this was an encounter. The turtle and I, we actually met. We eyeballed each other. If it could have talked it would have talked to me.

Her shell was covered in barnacles. With her weight and size, I guessed her age could be well in excess of 100 years. I say "her" because females tend to live longer. She may have seen square-rigged sailing ships in this ocean in the 19th century.

When you are on your own and have been alone for several months and you come eye to eye with another animal as wild and majestic as this ancient turtle, thousands of miles from land, it is quite a privilege and a very moving experience. It was an occasion to savour and it was one of the most indelible experiences on this journey.

After a minute or so it came even closer to the boat and then dived under and I could hear it scraping under the hull. I let it go a few minutes then I thought it might be trying to scratch those barnacles off, so I trimmed the sails and moved away. I could see it in the water as I left. It looked as if it was going somewhere. It wasn't in a hurry.

Later, when the boat was being taken out of the water in Greenland, I saw there was weed growing on the copper plate that was the earth of the single side-band radio. It was the only part of the bottom of the boat that didn't have anti-fouling paint on it. I realised that was what the turtle was doing under there. It wasn't worried about the barnacles. It just wanted a feed.

13

WATER, WATER EVERYWHERE

Day after day, day after day,
We stuck, nor breath nor motion;
As idle as a painted ship
Upon a painted ocean.

Water, water, every where,
And all the boards did shrink;
Water, water, every where,
Nor any drop to drink.
—Samuel Coleridge, "The Rime of the Ancient Mariner"

I dropped a silver coin over the side of the boat and watched as it went down. It spun, glinting in the sunlight as far down as 100 metres. I could see it for ages, as much as a minute or two, before it finally sank out of sight.

In the doldrums the water is like glass, the sky is blue and it's hot. There's always a gentle swell, but the sea calms down when the wind drops. If there are fish you can see them.

This is the tropical convergence zone about three to five degrees latitude either side of the equator, in both the Atlantic and Pacific oceans, where the low pressure calms the prevailing winds of the Northern and Southern Hemispheres. With light or no wind, sailboats before the prevalence of engines could be trapped for weeks – as happened to the poor souls in Coleridge's "The Rime of the Ancient Mariner". It's a catch-22 because if there's no wind, you can't move away from the windless area. I was fortunate though. I got a gentle breeze and as I moved, of course, I moved away from the doldrums. I made about four to five knots, managing daily runs of just over 100 miles. A slower yacht could have got stuck.

To some extent I was lucky, but on the other hand I had planned my course on the basis of the chance of getting favourable wind, so it was good management as well. Luck and good management are a good combination. I consider I was pretty lucky going around South Africa; and indeed the doldrums were kind to me as well.

In this area tides are stagnant and lots of rubbish congregates. I saw a lot of rubbish on my trip, especially going into the Northern Hemisphere, where you get eddies and currents mixing, so any rubbish will go on the tide line, drift across to one area and get pressed into one area. It can end up in a line that stretches for miles, maybe five to 10 metres wide, of rubbish – plastic of all sorts, bottles, jandals. I didn't come across the great areas they talk about – the North Atlantic and North Pacific garbage patches, where huge areas of rubbish are all packed together, but I definitely noticed that as I entered the Northern Hemisphere the rubbish seemed to collect on the tides and currents. Anything heavy sinks. I personally don't have too much of an issue with glass because it's going back to where it came from. But plastic, when it breaks down in the sunlight, disintegrates into ever-smaller particles while remaining a polymer, toxic to birds and fish.

Where it's congested you see it clearly, but you see it generally, too, every day, just stuff in the water. Then days can go by when you don't see anything. I guess if it keeps moving it will eventually wash up on a beach somewhere, and maybe that's the best thing – to wash up and get collected. I thought about how some years previously I'd been sailing in Tahiti near an atoll called Rangiroa. Walking on the outside of the reef on the sandy beach I really felt I was in the most remote part of the world, and yet there were dozens of jandals lying all along the shore. There were so many of them I could probably have found a pair matched left and right and in the same colour.

Of course, there's no line where the equator is, but once you shift across it and into the Northern Hemisphere you do notice a difference – not only the rubbish, but more shipping, more aircraft and a shift in the quality of the air.

Half of the world's population lives north of 27 degrees N, and from my observation this is where the air and water is dirty. It seems clear that overpopulation creates pollution.

I was concerned that during the previous months I may have picked up weed, rope or netting on the keel. The boat was sailing well and I didn't have any reason to believe there was anything on there, but I wanted to be sure. So one afternoon when the wind died away I decided to go over the side. I dropped the sail quickly, put my snorkel on, tied myself to the boat and climbed over the back. It was my first time in the water. I wasn't keen. I was nervous about leaving the boat.

I was prepared to swim under to have a look but by holding on and just putting my head under I could easily see there was nothing wrong.

The water was crystal clear. It's hard to know how far you can see – probably 300–400 metres when it changes colour. As you look along the water to the horizon it's quite light and as you look down it's crystal clear. But then as you look down further into the abyss it almost goes black. It would be two or three kilometres deep at that point.

It all just took me half a minute and then I climbed sprightly back on board to my sanctuary. The temperature out of the water was 32 degrees so the dip was quite refreshing. I could have gone for a swim, but I didn't want to let go of the boat.

I suppose sharks were also a reason not to linger. The chances were probably a million to one but it would be a bit silly if I went for a swim and got eaten by a shark after all that preparation.

———

Around this time I talked by phone to my friend Stan Pearson, with whom I sailed the Melbourne to Osaka two-man race in 1987. Stan was based in Antigua and ran Antigua Rigging. Having lived there for many years and being a keen sailor, he has a great knowledge of the hurricane season. The hurricanes spawn in the west of Africa in the desert. They're an air mass that rises up into a squall or thunderhead, and as they move across the Atlantic some of them disappear but others gain momentum to create havoc when they hit the Caribbean. Some were drifting across, Stan told me, and one was behind me. That one would be called Harvey if it intensified.

But as it was moving west and I was moving north I was not too concerned.

———

Meanwhile, I was approaching the Sargasso Sea. This is a vast area covered with Sargasso seaweed, a floating mass of orangey-brown algae that stretches across an area 900 nautical miles wide and 2000 long, from roughly 70°–40° west and 20°–25° north, although I saw it in the water much further north than this. The Sargasso is the only sea without a land boundary, and exists within the North Atlantic. I started noticing the weed when I picked it up on the fishing lure. Within days it looked so thick I could walk on it, but with no roots it is simply floating on top of the water. It doesn't appear to affect sailing.

The breeze picked up as I escaped the equator region, and I was back to averaging 160 miles per day. Many squalls blew over, and I was able to collect plenty of rainwater, happy to have full water tanks (now about 146 litres) as I had been down to 15 days of bottled water (30 if rationed).

As I sailed out of the Sargasso Sea, I passed day 100 of my voyage, having travelled 15,000 miles around the planet.

———

Now that I was in the Northern Hemisphere I began to notice more shipping. Tankers travelled between Africa and America – three all at once on one day, which was a little unnerving. I might have been all alone out here, and yet in some ways I was right in the thick of the world economy. Tankers were coming from Nigeria filled with oil en route to the United States. Others were coming back, full of who knows what.

I was on autopilot so I just held my course. I figured if they saw I was holding my course they could make any adjustments they needed to. It's better to stay on your course if you've got the ship on your port side. Regardless of whether you're sailing or not, you've got the right of way. You give way to your right, and anything on the left you don't have to give way to.

Having said that, though, in a small boat you give way to whatever you have to give way to. You avoid an accident. There's a saying that power gives way to sail, but I disagree with that. If you're a 10-tonne boat and there's a 100,000-tonne boat coming along, it's easier for you to give way. I did that in the Pacific at one stage where the biggest container ship I'd ever seen in my life was steaming along. It looked as if it had a full cargo going from the United States to China. I reckoned it was doing 25 knots and it was so enormous it would have taken half a day to change course. I wasn't going to take the chance that it was going to give way to me. I just went about, let it go through and carried on.

Early August and I was really starting to focus on the Arctic, which was now 2500 miles away. I had started my Arctic checklist and was working through it. I was always making checklists – they're about foreseeing problems, preparing for what's to come, preventive measures essentially. On my Arctic list were: fit the anchor on bow, check clothing, gloves, goggles, hat, sleeping bags, wet-weather gear, oil keel and try to lift when calm. I was checking weather forecasts for that area, and was in contact with Peter Semotiuk, who operated a radio service out of Cambridge Bay, about halfway through the Northwest Passage, and also with the Canadian Coastguard. The news was good – ice was expected to break up by the end of the month in Peel and Larsen Sounds.

Meanwhile I was getting good winds. I hadn't run my engine for more than a week because my alternative charging systems were working so well.

I was still getting updates from Stan in Antigua who told me Harvey had turned into a hurricane and was sweeping the Caribbean, expected to veer north. I would have to watch out for this.

I also had the help of Team NZ weather guru Rodger ("Clouds")

Badham. I was getting texts from him throughout the journey, and my family at home gave me regular, invaluable information.

I caught my biggest fish so far. I had taken about 10 so far to eat, most of them small enough to allow me to take a quick fillet off each side to eat straight away. But this tuna was too large for that so I filleted one side and left the remainder in the cockpit. The next morning I took a fillet off the other side and enjoyed a late lunch. By about 5pm I felt tired and lay down, noticing a tingling sensation in my feet. It soon spread to my hands and I knew I was in trouble. Food poisoning.

I had made a pretty stupid mistake in leaving the tuna out overnight in 25 degrees. Fish needs to be kept cool, but I'd given the bacteria in that tuna the perfect opportunity to flourish. It was my own fault and I should have known better.

At 9pm it started raining and it was necessary to erect the rainwater collection sheet. In 20-knot winds, with me being half naked and needing to rush below every two to three minutes, it was neither an ideal scenario nor a pretty sight.

It took 20 hours to clean me out, and I am glad there was no reality TV around.

By the following afternoon, with a completely flushed out body, I felt weak. But then I started to feel hungry and soon I was back to normal. Great how the body solved the problem, albeit a little uncomfortably.

14

THE WRATH
OF HARVEY

"Wouldst thou," – so the helmsman answered,
"Learn the secret of the sea?
"Only those who brave its dangers
"Comprehend its mystery!"
—Henry Wadsworth Longfellow, "The Secret of the Sea"

By this stage, Cyclone Harvey had already caused havoc through the Caribbean and then barrelled up the east coast of the United States, swamping New York. I listened on the news, but I didn't have access to the weather maps and couldn't see exactly where he'd got to now. I was confident I was sailing away from it.

Stan and my shore advisors told me I should consider slowing down to be sure of letting it pass in front of me – but that went against everything that I had done so far, trying to push hard to be on time further north. I figured I'd be well out of Harvey's way. These hurricanes didn't usually come as far north as I now was.

And I was making great progress. Wind was freshening from the southwest and I'd had a blustery night sailing at 8–10 knots, peaking at 17.5 knots, with two reefs in the main. By morning the skies were dark and the tailwind that I had been running with started to ease off. It dropped right away by about 8am so I decided to shake the reef out and go with the full main.

I was up by the mast and had just hoisted the sail to the top when I saw, in the opposite direction, water lifting off the sea surface in a pattern that was heading my way fast. I had just enough time to lower the mainsail and tie it to the boom when *wham*, I was hit by a hurricane-force wind of between 75 and 85 knots. I had sailed into the centre of Hurricane Harvey. Here he was, further north than I'd believed him to be, at 40°05' west 43°04' north.

I was so lucky it hadn't arrived a minute or two earlier. If I hadn't been able to instantly get the sail down, Harvey would have blown it right out. The boat sat with no sail up as the storm went through.

I hadn't been able to see exactly where the storm was. It could have been 40 miles to one side or the other and I might have been on the edge of the eye and just had strong winds all the time. In saying that, the eye of the storm is an area of no wind at all as the cyclone turns around it, and the wind direction changes depending on where you are across that eye. When you go through a storm like that it's got an area on one side that's quite wide. It could be 100 miles wide, but on the other side is a narrow band but with stronger wind – perhaps five times the velocity as on the other side – and that's what I sailed into.

It was off the scale. At its strongest I guessed 85–90 knots, which is over 100 miles an hour, or around 170 kilometres an hour. It could have been 10 on either side. It was blowing so hard I couldn't stand up without holding on. I just held on. Mostly I was inside the boat or hatchway. If I was on deck I held on or crawled.

It lasted maybe six or seven hours, blowing so hard I knew it couldn't blow for long. It was moving on, and I just had to hold on.

In conditions like that the sea is blown around so much that it feels as if it's raining all the time. Wave caps are white from being whipped around. The waves weren't especially high to begin with, but the problem with the wind coming up so quickly was that the seas were close together. That was the danger. If they rose big and close that's when you got into trouble. I knew that if I got two together I could roll.

I wasn't scared but I was concerned. I had plans to follow, and that kept me logical and methodical. My rule for situations like this is to stay with what you've got. *You've prepared something so stay with it, trust it.* Trust the boat, trust the design, trust the skill that's gone into building it. Trust the equipment. Trust all the planning that has got you to this point.

Fear comes when you're out of control. I was in a dangerous situation but I was in control. I had options. I had plans and I moved through them.

Plan A was to lie a-hull with the wind and seas coming from the port side. This is one way of weathering a storm, by downing all sail, locking the tiller to leeward and going with the storm. But it was such an incredible wind this quickly proved impossible. The seas were starting to rise and I knew if it went on like that, she would roll.

Plan B: I tried running off, but even without any sail up the yacht was moving too fast and would pitch pole. I went back to lying a-hull, which meant letting the boat drift sideways at about 1.5 knots with the wheel locked hard over and the seas just washing underneath. But as time went on the sea got bigger, and if it got too much bigger there was a chance it could have turned me right over. That's what I was preparing for.

I stood in the doorway, wet-weather gear on, ready to close the watertight door if she rolled.

It was definitely scary with the wind screaming around me, but my knees were not knocking. I was as prepared as I could be with everything inside tied down that I could manage, although if there's a rollover you get a hell of a mess. It would roll over and it would come back up. Chances are the mast could break if it rolled over. I might lose rigging. But I thought that if the boat had rolled it would have rolled over quite well. Its keel was deep, it would have done the thing, but it would be silly to sit there and let it roll again. You'd have to do something to hold it into the wind, and that's how I got to Plan C.

Plan C: I had a sea anchor that I'd bought in the local marine shop the day before I left Auckland. It was a large canvas cone like a small parachute that when lowered into the water acts like a brake and helps to hold the boat in a desired position. I tied a long rope to it and crawled up the deck to the front. I had my harness on, and a lifeline all the way up the front.

If I had just let the sea anchor go it would have flown like a kite in the 85-knot wind. So I bunched the thing up, lay flat on the deck, leant over the front and threw it vigorously down into the water. It drifted away. I had the rope cleated to the bow and when tight the water filled the canvas cone and the bow started to come around and head into the wind. Perfect, I thought.

But then the ropes attached to the sea anchor broke loose and all grip was lost. I discarded it in frustration and crawled along the deck back to the relative safety of the cockpit.

The seas were getting dangerous. The waves seemed to be sliding underneath, but if two waves broke close to each other I was sure she would roll.

Plan D: The rope ladder used for going up the mast could be used as a drogue in the water, especially if looped. So this was my next move: to unpack it on the cockpit floor, take it to the bow and use it to try and do the same job as the sea anchor in order to hold the boat head-on to the wind and waves. I had my head down, unpacking the ladder as waves crashed against and over me, but I looked up for a minute and happened to glance to windward where I noticed a thin sliver of blue sky on the horizon. I knew instantly that this would be the end of the blow. I just needed to hold on.

The horizon is 12 miles away, so whatever speed Harvey was moving at I knew the end was in sight. But it seemed to take a long time.

Plan E, and I was not sure how many plans I had left. Even with no sails up, the mast and the rigging were enough for the wind to keep the boat heeled over.

Sometimes a storm will be so bad that a crew will actually take the rig off to survive. They'll undo the rigging and drop the mast and let it go over the side, or chop it down and get rid of it. Without the mast up you haven't got that wind leverage pushing the boat over.

It wasn't something I had got around to considering. I guess if the boat had rolled over and I couldn't do anything but let it roll over again, I might have considered dropping the rigging. It would have been a huge loss, though, and it's dangerous.

It would have been very hard on *Astral Express* to drop the rigging. The mast goes through the deck into the base and it's got ropes on it. You'd have to get the knife out and cut everything, get the bolt cutters out and chop the wire rigging off, and hope the mast would break cleanly. But there would be no guarantee of that. Then you'd need it all to just disappear cleanly over the side. It would be a real mess, and very difficult on my own.

If it had got to the stage where I thought forget the trip, forget keeping everything intact, it's a matter of survival here, I would probably have gone straight to Plan F.

I had, of course, been contemplating Plan F: escaping on the life raft. Getting the life raft out and inflated. It would not have been easy. To put it in the water and try and jump in would have been almost impossible. In this extreme wind it would have behaved like a kite and taken off before I could even get it over the side. How would I manage it? I figured I'd inflate it in the cockpit, keep it tied on and sit in it. Then if the boat rolled or sank I could untie it and it would float off. That would be the only way to evacuate, with grab bag at hand. It's called Plan F for a reason, because that's the point where you're f . . .

Then came a time when I knew in my bones the wind was dropping, although it seemed to take a long time. Ever so slowly it would ease off, only to come back again in force. But after some time the sliver of blue sky got larger and the wind eased and I lived to tell the tale.

The only damage I could find was that the sun and spray cover in the cockpit was a little torn, although it could be easily repaired with tape. And there were a few frayed nerves. An experience like that is physically exhausting, even though there was quite a bit of time when I wasn't doing much. I had no sails up. I had the wheel tied over to one side on lock and I just had to stand there letting it happen, eating food that I didn't have to cook or prepare such as biscuits or chocolate, and drinking water.

I was a bit disappointed I'd got into that situation by not holding back. Chances were that if I'd not kept going as fast I had, trying to beat Harvey, it would have just passed in front of me. I had been given advice to slow up, but I'd felt that with that tailwind I was going fast enough to sail through and would beat it. But then while it turned out to be prudent advice that I should hold back, the people back home didn't know exactly where the storm was, or where I was either.

My mistake came from not having a weather map on board at that particular time, because as it turned out, the tailwind was the other part of the storm. It moves in a circular motion and I was getting a tailwind then had sailed through the centre of it and encountered the headwind, which was more intense but luckily didn't last as long.

But as the wind died away I mostly felt relief that it hadn't lasted too long. I was glad it was over, and I was happy in the knowledge that the boat had passed its first real test. I knew now what it could stand. That was good knowledge to have once I was facing the Bering Sea because although the seas would be bigger there, the wind would not be as strong and I now knew the boat was able to handle what was dished out there.

I got everything tidied up. I put things away – lifejackets and wet-weather gear, my grab bag which had been all ready to go. Re-packed the life raft, re-packed the ladder. I'd had everything tied down below so that if I rolled over things wouldn't fly around, so I tidied all that up and got it back to normal. The sun came out and the boat dried out and we were back on the journey again.

If you're going to sail around the world, if you're going to cover 28,000 miles and be at sea for 190 days, chances are something's going to give you a hurry-up. I wrote a poem about my experiences:

> The breeze is gone, the breeze is gone.
> There's a line of blue on the horizon.
> The reef is out the head is full,
> The memory of the storm is fading from the sea.
> And now this is the best place to be.
> Unlike the gale in all its fury
> Venting foam and crashing waves,
> With rising wind and nervous tension
> This part of life is not worth a mention.

As I came into the trade winds I had squalls coming through every three or four hours. Like a thunderhead, the wind would increase suddenly about 5 to 10 knots, usually bringing rain. They didn't last long though – if I decided to have a wash, by the time I'd lathered up it would be gone.

Of my two rainwater-collection systems, one took about 10 minutes to set up, which wasn't suitable for a squall, and was difficult to manage in the wind anyway. But the other system worked well in these conditions. The dodger in the cockpit had a little hole in the middle of it with a screw cap in it so I could attach a hose from there straight into a water bottle. It was ready to go straight away, and a few minutes of heavy rain was enough to collect up to 10 litres of freshwater, which was enough to use for washing or topping up.

Squalls were just something I had to live with. They showed up well on the radar, so the radar alarm would go off when one was about eight miles away. I'd set the boat up, reduce sail, or just steer the boat downwind a bit, alter course 10 or 15 degrees for 20 minutes and then get back on course.

———

I realise a lot of people would be freaked out at the idea of sailing through a storm of the magnitude of Cyclone Harvey. People have asked me how I handled it. I think it comes down to having an optimistic nature. If you had a pessimistic nature you wouldn't do what I did. You wouldn't untie the boat to begin with. Sure, I ask, what are the odds of something bad happening? What are the odds of dying? I temper my optimism with experience and planning and I trust my own processes and the skills of the team I've built up around me. Mental attitude has a big part to play.

Some people turn to God when they're in extreme and dangerous circumstances. That's not how it works for me. I think "God" is a word that expresses the limits of our understanding – it's a word for the unknown.

We're taught where things come from; we know where that gadget comes from, how it was made. We know how we are made. But we can't work out where the universe comes from. That "somewhere" is where the word God comes into use – so God is an unknown. The unknown.

When you're out on the ocean alone, you do get philosophical. You see nature in all its extremes, and there you are in the middle of it all. When I was younger I was so busy doing stuff, knocking myself around, thinking I was infallible. But as I get older I think it's pretty amazing that we're here at all. How does it all work? It's just so incredible. Take the human body: for 60 years it's been working, the knees, the heart, the hands. Never been for a service. Never been for an oil and grease. I give it sleep and food but other than that it just keeps working. I guess I have a sense of wonder about it, and maybe that awareness becomes stronger as I get older. People say, what do you think the most amazing thing is and I say, this: this hand. This ocean.

———

I sailed right over the spot where the *Titanic* went down in the North Atlantic at around 41 degrees latitude. There wasn't a bump; no deckchairs floated on the surface. I looked around and all I could see was ocean – blue, blue ocean. No icebergs at this time of year, and a long way south for icebergs even in winter. The ship rests four kilometres down. I don't think anyone ever calls their ship unsinkable now. I *thought* Astral Express was unsinkable – but I certainly never said it was.

———

At 15 weeks into my journey, Lancaster Sound was less than 2000 miles away. I was making 150 miles a day, meaning I was 13.5 days away. It was now 11 August, so I thought I would make it on time.

I was in the Labrador Sea 350 miles from Newfoundland, sailing ENE to avoid two low-pressure systems ahead when I began receiving news that tropical storm Irene was approaching from the south. It had already drenched New York and was on its way to causing havoc in the United Kingdom. I hoped I was far enough north, but I felt as if I was between a rock and a hard place. I needed to be at 57° north by Thursday 18 August, but perhaps it wasn't to be: on Friday, the NNW gale caught me. There I was in the centre of the Labrador Sea as the 45-knot gale set in. I had to run off and move south, then lie a-hull again to slow the progress in the wrong direction.

I was getting close to Canada and starting to acknowledge that if this weather carried on I was not going to make it in time up to Lancaster Sound. I began to think about where I would go if I couldn't make the Northwest Passage, and I figured the choice was between St John's at the eastern tip of Newfoundland or Nuuk, the capital of Greenland.

But then thankfully the storm moved off and I was able to get back on course. The chart shows where I went during Irene – it's an almost perfect circle, out there in the middle of the Labrador Sea. That's the thing with modern technology – everyone at home could see what I was doing. They got up and looked at their computers and saw where I was, and someone asked, "Why did you go around in circles?" I said, "I lost my hat!"

That 2005 hurricane season was the most active on record with 28 storms, most of them hurricanes. It didn't stop with Harvey and Irene. Soon after came Hurricane Katrina, which, of course, devastated part of the United States and became one of the costliest natural disasters in history.

Goodbye Irene! By Saturday evening the gale was subsiding and by Sunday the birds were back around the boat as usual. Time for a party – a shave and drinks.

I hadn't used the engine since before Harvey and the wind generator had been working overtime.

Water temperature was now nine degrees. Things were really cooling down and as I passed through 60° north on Monday, between Canada and the west coast of Greenland, I was on iceberg watch. I had seen no land since the Cape of Good Hope.

I was now approaching Davis Strait with Lancaster Sound about 600 miles away and Bellot Strait another 350 miles. Ice reports were saying that Bellot Strait and Peel Sound should be ice-free by the end of August. I had time to get there.

I spent a lot of time studying my charts of the area. I carried a full set of charts for the Northwest Passage from the Canadian Hydro Office. Although electronic charts for my course were supplied with the chart plotter, I felt it wise to have paper back up and found these necessary for studying the course ahead. Electronic charts had only just become available for the part of the Arctic I was about to sail through. I did have this advantage over previous explorers.

15

THE UNANSWERABLE ICE

Like the winds of the seas are the ways of fate,
As we voyage along through the life:
Tis the set of a soul
That decides its goal,
And not the calm or the strife.
—Ella Wheeler Wilcox, "The Winds of Fate"

On Tuesday 23 August I sailed into Davis Strait with an escort of northern bottlenose whales. About six of them swam either side of the boat, at the back. They accompanied me for a day, and every now and again one would swim up until it was alongside me, about three metres away. When I stood inside looking forward I could see out of the corner of my eye these huge animals swimming alongside. But as soon as I turned my head to look at them in the eye, they retreated. This happened several times, always with the same result. It was like a game. They'd swim up, I'd pretend not to notice, and then as soon as I looked, they'd drop back.

It was really starting to cool off now at 64° north, getting close to freezing. Sitting out in the cockpit, enjoying the weak afternoon sun, I observed the dozens of planes – 30 or 40 of them in an afternoon – that flew west from Europe to America over Greenland, the Arctic and Canada. As I sat there, six flew over in quick succession within a 10-minute period, leaving white contrails in the sky. Within 30 minutes the upper wind had merged the contrails into a cloud and the sun faded and the temperature dropped; time to put a jacket on. It was a small, personal experience of the overall effect of the temperature change caused by this by-product of aviation.

———

On Wednesday 24 August I sailed into the Arctic Circle at 66°33' north, approaching Baffin Bay. Hundreds of icebergs lay ahead, scattered like islands across the ocean as far as the eye could see, the most magnificent shapes and colours I had ever seen. There was one every five miles or so and always 10 to 15 in sight at any one time – massive things, 20, 30, 40 metres high with the craggy sea ice about four to five metres high surrounding them.

If you take a bird's-eye view of the top of the globe, the Arctic Circle hoops around the North Pole with a radius of almost 1600 miles. It marks the southernmost latitude in the Northern Hemisphere at which the sun can remain above or below the horizon for 24 hours. The period of the midnight sun had occurred in the last two weeks of June, but by the time I arrived in the area the days were still over 21 hours long, with the sun dipping below the horizon between 11.30pm and 2am. That was lucky, as navigation was now so important and difficult. I was grateful for my spotlight and also my night-vision binoculars, through which the white of the smaller icebergs showed up vividly.

Originating from the glaciers of western Greenland, the icebergs calve off into the sea and drift northwards until they meet the Labrador current, which then takes them south towards Newfoundland and into the North Atlantic. They can float for years, the wind and currents carving Byzantine shapes and angles into them, making them sometimes impossible to detect using radar.

While the larger ones generally showed up, at some angles they simply didn't reflect the radar signal. Vigilance was essential. I would do a visual count, then a radar count, and one or two would always be missing until I got closer to them, or even actually passed them, when a good radar signal would appear as the shape changed.

They changed shape from every angle. Majestic, beautiful works of art. I sailed over to one large berg in order to have a better look and was amazed at its many incredible shapes and colours. I could see vivid green and blue crevasses and the most artistic shapes imaginable. And it was so flat on top you could land an aircraft on it.

However, I didn't get too close. When I was a kilometre from it I could see clearly that much of it was underwater. I knew that if pieces broke off, which they often did, chunks the size of trucks falling without warning into the sea, the berg would become unstable and easily tip over, the underwater part rushing into the air. I wouldn't want to be sailing over it if that happened.

No two parts or sides of an iceberg are the same, and no two icebergs are the same. Each bit of an iceberg weathers in its own way, from the effects of wind, rain, sun and sea. They are spectacular yet at the same time a little daunting to sail through.

Ice was blocking the western part of Baffin Bay and with the entrance at Lancaster Sound now only a day or two away I bore off to the east to avoid the ice sheet.

―――――――――

The news was now not positive. Several boats were waiting in Cambridge Bay. They had come into the Northwest Passage from the west, but their course to the east was blocked.

Skip Novak, the famous Whitbread yachtsman and adventurer, was also up in the Arctic, hoping to take a group of tourists through the Northwest Passage aboard his boat *Pelagic Australis*. He told me by radio that he wasn't able to get into Lancaster Sound. He had retreated to Bylot Island to go climbing instead.

Canadian Coastguard confirmed that conditions were not good this season for the Northwest Passage transit. Although total ice area was low, wind had caused it to congest the Canadian side of the Arctic. It was unlikely to open this year.

The people I talked to by radio were amazed at what I'd done – leaving Auckland in April and making it with perfect timing up to the Northwest Passage in late August. I took some heart in that. I had designed my journey correctly, and that in itself was an achievement.

By this stage I was up over 70° north and by the afternoon of 26 August it was becoming obvious it was no use carrying on. The ice wasn't going to clear. But I wasn't ready to turn around and I sailed on northwards for another day, giving it time to sink in and hoping for a miracle. But there was to be no miracle.

With ice continuing to block the entrance, there was no way through. Only an icebreaker could make it.

It was pretty obvious it was a no go. It was going to get worse, not better. I knew I had to let it go, this dream of sailing the Northwest Passage.

If I carried on I would risk getting trapped and not being able to retreat. Spending a dark winter on board was not something I would relish, even though the *Astral Express* was designed and set up for such an eventuality.

By early Saturday morning, just up into Baffin Bay and a day and a half away from Lancaster Sound, the time came to make the final decision. After 24 hours of facing the reality, I accepted it. You can't sail through ice. At that moment of letting go, I was sailing on starboard tack in really light winds, about 10 knots. The boat was doing about three or four knots. It was a nice morning. There was a little bit of sea running. The sails were tight and I was sailing hard on the wind when along came a little wave and, without me touching it, the headsail went about by itself, as if it had made the decision for me.

Well, I said to myself, *there you go. This is it.* So I just let it go – I changed the sails, got the auto-pilot up and made a new course, away from Lancaster Sound.

Where was I going to go? I had no Plan B. I revisited the options I'd considered during Hurricane Irene. St John's? Or Nuuk? The more I thought about it, the more logical it seemed. I set my course for Nuuk, about 130 miles away.

This is what I wrote in my log at the time:

"It is with heavy heart that I have made the decision not to proceed further towards the Northwest Passage. The conditions ahead are now too dangerous and I can't go against nature and common sense. The plan now is to head south out of the icebergs and make for Nuuk, the capital of Greenland . . .

"After four months at sea and 18,000 miles it is disappointing to change direction but the cup is always half full. A new era will unfold with a visit to such an exciting country as Greenland, and it's also comforting that some kids throughout the world might benefit in some small way because of my adventure."

Of course, it was disappointing to have come so far and not be able to complete the total plan. But I couldn't argue with the ice. There was absolutely nothing I could have done differently to have brought about a different outcome, and so I actually felt comfortable. Rather than any sense of failure, I had a tremendous feeling of success.

Nuuk is also known as Godthab, meaning "good hope". Landfall to landfall, I'd sailed from Good Hope to Good Hope – 8,600 nautical miles – almost as far as you can go in a straight line without landfall at sea on this planet.

I'd sailed a total of 18,000 miles. I was in one piece. The boat was in one piece. I'd enjoyed the journey.

It's *fate*, I said to myself. Fate had delivered this result. I accepted that.

16

A SILVER LINING

When the wind fades away
And the fish stay at bay
When the rain you need never comes
The clouds obscure the sun and the sea turns grey
You wished you'd sailed around the world another day.
—Graeme Kendall

According to the Icelandic Sagas, it was the Viking Eric the Red who first gave Greenland its whimsical name. It was a marketing ploy. He was hoping it would attract settlers, as indeed it did. But actually Greenland is mostly ice caps and glaciers, and is the source of most of the icebergs in the Arctic Circle.

Greenland glacier calving is so prevalent because physically Greenland is like a bowl – a rocky bowl – much of it pressed below sea level by the weight of a huge ice dome. In 1992 an ice core was drilled from this dome, and it was found to be 3028 metres deep. The ice dome is like a scoop of ice cream on a cone dripping into the ocean. The weight of the ice dome, coupled with wave erosion at the water line, erodes crevasses into the ice dome, causing calving and fracturing.

Most of the population of Greenland live around the habitable fringe of the country, mostly among the fjords in the southwest coast.

Nuuk is situated down a fjord on the west coast of Greenland on a rocky promontory. With a population of 16,000 it is the smallest capital in the world and the most northerly, sitting right at the edge of the Arctic Circle. With just over a day's sailing time to arrive there, I had time to collect my thoughts and make some new plans. I tidied and cleaned up the boat, and tidied myself ready for human contact and the next – unexpected – phase of the journey.

After speaking to family and friends about the situation, I contacted Nuuk Harbour Control to let them know of my arrival and request a favourable berth. Within a few hours, the Nuuk TV station called me to ask if two reporters could come out to meet me at the entrance to the fjord. They wanted to interview me about the solo voyage from New Zealand to Greenland. This was convenient, as my charts were not detailed enough for the passage through the waterway to Nuuk. It was agreed that Jesper the station manager would bring the TV crew on his private boat out to meet me at the heads, and I could then follow him back on the two-hour cruise up to Nuuk.

By Sunday morning, with slight seas, *Astral Express* made the ETA of 10am to rendezvous with the television crew. Two very pleasant local people came aboard. We soon settled with question time over a cup of coffee, him filming and her interviewing. They slipped easily between the three languages – Danish, as Greenland is part of Denmark's domain, and Inukitut, which is the local Inuit language, and they spoke good English.

I'd had an email from the harbour control telling me where to berth, and with Nuuk in sight the TV crew departed in order to be at the dock when I stepped off the boat. They obviously wanted to see if I could walk straight.

With all sails furled and the boat tided up I slowly motored into the marina. Nuuk is extremely pretty as you approach it from the sea. Its colourful houses dot the hillsides in red, yellow and blue, standing out against the rocky slopes. On the other side of the fjord, massive mountains loom, and the icy waters throw brilliant reflections.

Let's call it a wrap, I said to myself.

To my surprise, a large group of people were waiting for me, including the Mayor. I stepped gingerly ashore and to everyone's surprise, including my own, I was able to walk straight without wobbling. I was welcomed to Nuuk by the Mayor and presented with small gifts.

By that stage it was about 2 o'clock on a summer's afternoon.

Back on board, several people dropped by to have a look at *Astral Express* and to chat about my journey. One of them was a schoolteacher who was also an enthusiastic sailor. He asked me, speaking good English, if he could help or do anything for me.

While I was still unsure of my next step, I told him I'd been thinking of shipping the boat back to Auckland. My thinking was that I would try to sell her there. I asked this fellow if he knew of a local company that could haul the boat out and arrange shipping. He said the only company that he knew was Nuuk Transport and that I should contact Edward Niclasen. He gave me the phone number.

I stayed on board that night. I had my usual dinner, and noted how odd it was with no movement of the boat. I was still coming to terms with how things had turned out. It all felt quite strange, but I felt inside myself the scale of my achievement, even without having been able to tackle the Northwest Passage. Eighteen thousand miles was great, and I knew I could have continued. My fuel tanks were almost half full. Everything was in such perfect condition I had no need to go to the marine store. I had plenty of food and didn't need to visit the supermarket. The only thing I was low on was wine – I was down to my last bottle and I joked to family that was my reason for calling the trip off.

The next morning I rang Edward Niclasen of Nuuk Transport, and he came down to *Astral Express* that afternoon. Edward is a big man, very pleasant and practical, and it's funny to think that as we shook hands I had no idea of how important he was to become in my story. I welcomed him on board, showed him my floating home and told him of my plan. Edward was keen to help me.

Next day we visited several shipping offices, including his own, and it soon became clear that getting back to Auckland would prove expensive and complicated. *Astral Express* would need to have a cradle built for safe transportation. The journey back to New Zealand would mean transferring between two or three ships at different ports, meaning there were security concerns. I realised I might have to cut the mast in half to save $40,000 shipping costs, and I got in contact with Philip Wilson back in Auckland to discuss exactly where on the mast would be the best place to cut.

I didn't think I had any option. I considered then dismissed the idea of sailing back myself. It wasn't in the plan. I wouldn't have enjoyed it.

Later that afternoon Edward came back on board and I gave him a more detailed tour. The boat was immaculate and I think Edward was impressed with this, especially considering that it had just sailed 18,000 miles from Auckland non-stop. Nothing was needed, no repairs required. She was still in great shape, ready to complete the planned attempt.

He thought it was a very good boat for the conditions in this part of the world. He asked what price I would be asking for her in Auckland. Then he said he could be interested in buying her. I said I would do my homework and come up with a favourable price for him in the morning, taking into account shipping costs and so on.

I rang an old friend back in New Zealand.

"I've got a man here wants to buy the boat," I told him.

"How much?" he asked.

I told him what I was thinking.

"Sell it," he said. "Walk away. Northwest Passage is shut. You're not getting through there. It's got nothing to do with you or your ability. It's closed. It's like going to the pub, mate. The door is shut. You have to go somewhere else. Sell it, mate."

Edward's offices and factory were on the waterfront and included a large cafeteria where most of the port workers gathered. Over breakfast there we discussed a deal and agreed on a figure. His requirements were to inspect the boat out of the water on Friday and a sea trial on Saturday.

To tell the truth, I was sceptical. What if he let me down or didn't buy it? I had booked tickets to fly out of Greenland the following Tuesday, so if he didn't buy I would be in trouble with time very tight to make other arrangements. *Hang on Graeme*, I said to myself. *Get a grip. Trust fate.*

It almost seemed too good to be true.

After three days in harbour, and now more confident that the sale would go through, I booked into the Hotel Hans Edege on Thursday. On Friday I took *Astral Express* around to the port near Nuuk Transport where Edward had one of his large crane trucks ready to lift her out of the water for inspection. The lifting keel had got stuck and Edward wanted to see it working, which he did, and the rest of the boat looked perfect underneath. That test passed, she was back in the water ready for a sea trial the next day.

I did enjoy the steak and wine at the hotel that night, but I was lonelier in the hotel than I had been on the boat. Nuuk seemed like a town on Mars, utterly foreign to me, although I would get to know it under very different circumstances a few years later.

Saturday was partly cloudy with light winds and the odd iceberg floating down the summery fjord past Nuuk. Edward and a few friends came aboard and we enjoyed a sail around the bay. We could hear gunshots inland in the hills. Hunters shooting reindeer and muskox. When I asked them what they shoot in Greenland the reply was "Anything that moves". It is definitely not safe for a whale to stray into the bay.

I treated them to lunch from my menu of freeze-dried food and a beer, and we toasted a successful sail and sea trial.

And so the deal was done. We discussed the tricky matter of how to arrange payment and the transfer of ownership. A neutral lawyer would draw up an agreement on Monday, hold the funds in trust and release them to me upon proof of clear title that I would supply upon my return to New Zealand. Perfect.

We left the boat moored to the wharf by the factory and on Sunday Edward brought his family down to the boat. Birgit, his wife, who is a doctor and originally from Denmark, and their younger son Simun were there as Edward and I showed them around.

I had gathered together some small personal items to take home with me – my computer, camera, boots and a few clothes – but left everything else with the boat. As we were about to leave Edward asked if there was anything else I wanted to take. I thought and then said yes. I proceeded to the forward cabin and retrieved the Fedex box and Wilson that I had been given by Gareth Ramage the previous Christmas. Edward couldn't believe his eyes. He said that he'd looked over every inch of the boat and never saw the box.

And so I left *Astral Express*, walking away with scarcely more than a carry-on bag.

I was invited to the Niclasen house that evening. We had a great night with discussions about my voyage and stories of their family history.

Edward told me of his plans for *Astral Express*. He would put it in an air-conditioned shed during their winter and have some modifications done. He wanted to make her more cruising-oriented for him and his family to use, mainly opening up cabin space that I had used for watertight compartments or storage.

He was originally from the Faroe Islands, about 1500 miles to the east beyond Iceland, and the following year, 2006, was the Faroes' 100-year anniversary of sailing fishing boats. Edward wished to be there in his new vessel. I think it was really for this that he had bought *Astral Express*.

Towards the end of the night, a remarkable thing happened. He told me that if I wanted to complete my attempt at a later stage he would be happy to make the boat available. This gesture blew me away.

I thanked him very sincerely and said I would consider it. However, right at that moment I felt happy about what I had done and my thoughts had turned to home.

On Monday we concluded the paperwork and I was given more sightseeing drives around the town. Kids will be pleased to know that their Christmas mail goes to a large post box labelled "Postbrevkasse", about four metres high with a glass window, that stands right on the waterfront in Nuuk. That day in early September it was already about half full. The local schoolchildren reply to the mail.

That night, my final night in Greenland, I had dinner at Jesper's and watched the news feature they had put together on my arrival. It was amusing watching Jesper, whom I had previously seen only in his casual clothes and boating attire, announce the evening news on television wearing a jacket and tie and being all prim and proper. The first bulletin was at 6pm, presented in the Inukitut language, followed at 7pm with the Danish segment. When my item came on I couldn't understand a word – even my dialogue was translated. It was all quite bizarre, but nice to know that they deemed my trip so newsworthy. To have a New Zealander sail solo non-stop to Nuuk – this was a definite first.

By Tuesday it was time for farewells and I boarded the plane for the journey home, trying not to feel I had my tail between my legs. It was a far cry from being in my own cockpit in the wide open spaces of the ocean.

What a strange, whirlwind week this had just been. What were the odds of sailing to Nuuk – of even sailing a yacht up to Greenland – then of finding a buyer for that yacht? What were the odds of that buyer offering it back for use in the future?

———

Back in New Zealand, I prepared all the documentation and the sale of *Astral Express* was completed.

What I had achieved was precious and I accepted what fate had delivered.

17

INTERIM

'Tis evening on the moorland free,
    The starlit wave is still:
Home is the sailor from the sea,
    The hunter from the hill.
—A E Housman, "Home is the Sailor"

The grey, the dark, the deepness – the sea has no feeling for you. I didn't want Graeme to go away again. It was dangerous. Anything could happen. But there was no way he was going to give it up for me. And so I started to have the feeling that he should achieve something he really wanted to. I had to close the shutters of my heart and let him go.

—Franceska Marsic

During the first year at home I continued fundraising for Variety and the Christchurch Children's Hospital, mainly through charity luncheons where I could speak about my voyage. Reliving the events felt strange as the sailing itself had been such a private experience. However, following the solo 18,000-mile voyage I had returned with the feeling of being invulnerable. Bulletproof. No challenge could ever seem too great. I felt that if I could do what I had just done, I could handle any situation.

Meanwhile, on the other side of the globe, in 2006 *Astral Express* sailed to the Faroe Islands, Edward's original home, where his mother and brother live.

The following year I moved to Auckland, the sailing capital of the world, charged with a new direction in life. As things settled down, I started to think more about the offer that Edward had made that Sunday evening over dinner in Greenland.

I decided to take up his offer and try to complete the plan. I would do it in 2007. I booked my tickets to the Faroes where Edward was with *Astral Express*, then together we would sail to Nuuk and from there I would proceed solo to the Northwest Passage.

The night before I was due to fly out from New Zealand I was informed that Edward was in Faroe Hospital in Torshavn with a heart problem. Although his wife Birgit insisted I should still go, I felt I would want Edward with me for the week's journey to Nuuk to become familiarised with any changes made to the boat, and to have his help with preparation in Greenland.

I cancelled my tickets. Edward was subsequently treated and recovered.

The following year I had family commitments. Then in 2009 I also had heart problems, luckily not serious and treatable.

It now seemed that 2010 would be the year to continue my attempt to sail solo around the world, Auckland to Auckland via the Northwest Passage – albeit with a five-year gap.

This year suited both me and Edward. We decided to rendezvous in the Faroe Islands.

Ice reports from the Arctic between 2005 and 2010 showed continuing depletion during the summer months, with 2007 being the lowest ice areas recorded. By June of 2010 the ice reports looked favourable for another attempt that year. It would certainly be easier to judge the likelihood of getting through the Northwest Passage by seeing the conditions up there. I'd be leaving Nuuk in late August, not having to judge it from as far away as April as I had when leaving from Auckland in 2005.

I attended a one-month maritime school in Auckland during November 2009. You don't stay too complacent and I was trying to prepare myself in whatever way I could. I thought it was an opportunity to brush up on a few things. I did learn quite a lot – a bit of mechanical, engineering, navigation, buoys, first aid. I already knew about the mechanical stuff – the engines, batteries, alternators and so on – but you can always learn more. I ended up with a skipper's ticket which I then put in a drawer and forgot about, not foreseeing how useful it was going to be for me.

Now five years older, I concentrated on keeping fit, with sailing – I kept a 36-foot catamaran, *Te Mana*, up in Tahiti – and with weights and yoga at home. I was careful with my diet.

The previous voyage had come at a high financial cost with the sale price of *Astral Express* covering only about a third of its set-up cost, and now I required more to complete the trip. Air fares, communication costs, food, fuel, time off work – all these things had to be considered. But by now I had my heart set on completing what I'd started.

My partner Franceska didn't want me to go. She'd read a lot about the Northwest Passage and knew how dangerous it was. Meanwhile, I searched everywhere for my passport. Eventually I gave up and applied for a new one. Not long after that, Franceska confessed. She'd hidden it – her last attempt to get me to stay. It makes you realise how the wives of the sailors of old must have felt, with their men heading off for years and no possibility of news or communication.

We found a compromise. We would fly to London together, and then she would stay with her family in Croatia for the duration – for support, but also because she felt better being in the same hemisphere as me. It meant we could talk more easily. My day would be her day, my night her night. That way, she would feel a part of things.

18

THE ANCIENT MARINER HEADS BACK TO SEA

I must go down to the seas again, to the lonely sea and the sky,
And all I ask is a tall ship and a star to steer her by;
And the wheel's kick and the wind's song and the white sail's shaking,
And a grey mist on the sea's face, and a grey dawn breaking.

I must go down to the seas again, for the call of the running tide
Is a wild call and a clear call that may not be denied;
And all I ask is a windy day with the white clouds flying,
And the flung spray and the blown spume, and the sea-gulls crying.
—John Masefield, "Sea Fever"

As the small plane landed at Vagar airport in the Faroe Islands I felt the flutters of nervousness and excitement that meant I was on an adventure again.

This remote place is a small archipelago of 18 emerald islands scattered in the vast North Atlantic ocean at 62° north, midway between Norway and Iceland, about 4° south of the official boundary of the Arctic Circle, and almost 2000 kilometres to the east of Greenland. The Faroes are an autonomous country – in fact, Edward's brother Jorgen was Finance Minister in the Parliament – but they are within the Danish kingdom. Their history stretches back well over 1000 years, with a Viking settlement having been excavated beneath part of the village where Edward's mother lives.

It was to that village, Sorvagur, that I was taken from the airport by another of Edward's brothers. Edward himself was due to arrive on *Astral Express* the next day, Saturday.

It was a big weekend on the Faroes, being Olavsoka, the biggest midsummer festival on the islands, and celebrations were being held in the capital of Torshavn about 30 minutes' drive away. This is a three-day event and starts with the opening of the Faroese Parliament. The town goes mad with competitions and pop concerts. There's singing and dancing in the streets and most residents dress in national costume. For me it was quite surreal walking the main street at midnight in full daylight with partying going on.

Edward and family arrived aboard *Astral Express* the next morning. I was anxious to see what changes he had made to the boat. To my surprise she looked much the same as when I had left her. The front cabin was finished with double bed and teak lockers. The workshop area now had a bunk with a nicely built hinging shelf to serve as a workshop bench. The aft berth was finished and the whole interior now nicely lacquered. The navigation area, pipe berths and galley were the same as before. There was still no refrigeration. An extra diesel heater had been added. Little extra weight had been added and I was very impressed with what I saw.

That afternoon we were invited by Edward's brother Jorgen to a buffet lunch at the Parliament buildings where I met the Prime Minister and watched the traditional Viking boat racing from the balcony.

On Monday after the partying we prepared *Astral Express* for the cruise back to Nuuk in Greenland. This would be a trial for me to see how I felt about continuing – I was still prepared to ditch my plans had there been anything I didn't feel comfortable about.

Niclas, Edward's older son who had in the interim sailed and raced *Astral Express* in Denmark, accompanied Edward and me on the 1500-mile trip.

It was a bumpy ride, with several storms blowing in. We stopped briefly at Iceland to wait out a storm in the East Greenland Sea then proceeded to sail through Prince Christian Sound on the southern tip of Greenland, a narrow waterway of soaring pinnacles and glaciers – polar-bear territory, although we saw none. For most of the year it is clogged with pack ice but at that time it was clear for navigation except for the usual icebergs, with most stranded ashore. It was very beautiful and, like the rest of this journey, something to remember for the rest of my life.

We sailed up the west coast of Greenland after hitting a few pieces of drift ice. Edward was surprisingly keen to hit a bit of ice. He bought the boat knowing it would be ideal for it, but hadn't encountered much ice before, having been mostly sailing to the south of Greenland. He was pleased when the boat fended it off as designed. It was very unnerving when it happened, as I was resting below. Down there it sounded worse than it really was, a crashing, grinding, sliding sound. I rushed up only to find that the boat was fine. Not a mark on it. Despite the noise they were just small pieces.

It had taken a few days to get used to the boat again, but now I felt confident. The boat was in good shape. I felt I could do it. I wanted to give it a go. So on arriving at Nuuk it was down to business and time to prepare for the next major leg.

By this stage I was 63, so I wanted to be sure I could handle it. Put it this way: it's not that I was old. If you're going to live to 90, you're not old at sixty. But if someone had told me when I was 20 or 30 that when I was in my 60s I was going to sail around the world, I might have doubted it. Yet here I was, and I felt good. The fitness you need to sail is different from the fitness you need to run marathons. The best fitness I could get to prepare myself was to do some sailing, and so I'd taken a few catamaran sailing excursions in Tahiti. It was the best preparation, climbing up and down, being inside and out of a boat, grinding winches, pulling on halyards, working on a moving platform. I'd kept up with my yoga.

At the beginning of this second part of the trip I probably wasn't in as good a shape as I was back in 2005, but I soon got fit. By the time I'd sailed from the Faroe Islands to Nuuk I was starting to get in shape, and by the time I got to Lancaster Sound I was in pretty good shape. Then by the time I got back to New Zealand I was fit for the job. I couldn't have run a marathon but I was fit to sail.

Moored once more in the main port at Nuuk alongside the Nuuk Transport Building, I started the inevitable list of things to do. I had 10 days to prepare. It was now 9 August and I wanted to set sail for the Northwest Passage by about 18 August. This would allow me a week to sail across Baffin Bay towards the entrance of the Northwest Passage at Lancaster Sound, September being the ideal month to attempt the Northwest Passage with the lowest ice area at that time of the year. During August it was still melting and by October the sea would have started freezing again, soon to be totally blocked.

Ice reports looked promising so far. I would make a final decision to go in about seven days' time. One of Edward's brothers captained a very large Canadian fishing vessel which was in port, full of electronic communication equipment, and I was able to get good weather and ice information from him. I was receiving a coloured ice chart daily. The reports read like this:

Barrow – Lancaster – western half 4 tenths of first year ice including 1 tenth of old ice – Baffin Bergy water except 2 tenths of old ice. Ice edge near 68.25N to 70N. Sea ice west of the ice edge, etc.

Edward and Niclas were a great help, and together with them and one of their vehicles I was able to complete my short list of necessary supplies and start to provision the boat. The logistics for this were very different from what I'd had to do in Auckland. Leaving Auckland I had had to plan and ration everything for six months at sea. Now it was different. As I had already travelled 18,000 miles, all I had left was to sail across the top of Canada and Alaska and then down the full length of the Pacific – about 10,000 miles, or just over two months sailing time. In other words, just over half the length of the previous leg of the trip.

I could fill up on fuel, water, and fresh and frozen food. Helped by Birgit, Edward's wife, I went to the supermarket, grabbed a trolley and filled it with what I needed. Normal food. I had an icebox tied on the back of the boat that I stocked with meat, eggs, bacon, cheese – it was so cold back there it stayed like a refrigerator and everything lasted about five weeks. I didn't need the freeze-dried meals. I was able to take long-life milk, whereas on the first part of the trip I had powdered milk and just made up a bottle of milk every day for coffee and tea.

It was the same with drinks. I got a couple of dozen beers, a couple of bottles of rum. Everything was so much easier. The logistics of sailing for two months as opposed to six months were totally different.

Edward gave me a down-filled puffer jacket from his clothing store that was invaluable for the hours outside, although too warm to be worn inside. From the local fishermen's hardware store I bought plastic fur-lined boots and gloves at a fraction of the cost from a ski shop, and twice as good.

Birgit also helped me replenish the medical kit.

Edward had fitted a new communication system, so with two phone systems on board and the latest one fitted, getting ice and weather reports would now be quicker and less costly.

The nearby Nuuk Transport cafeteria was very convenient for meals and discussions. There was much interest in my plans, and the staff of Nuuk Transport and many others took a keen interest in proceedings. It was an exciting time, and I felt very comfortable and welcome in Nuuk.

Ice reports continued to look encouraging, but they were by no means certain. I was now fixed on a departure date of Thursday 19 August. The weekend before that I enjoyed a pleasant respite from busy planning when Edward invited me to accompany his family on a cruise through the fjords about 30 miles to spend a few days at their modest holiday home. This break was invaluable. I had time to relax, collect my thoughts and take my mind off the boat and what might lie ahead. We went hunting, caught trout in the stream and soaked up the remote picturesque environment, a part of the world few people have ever seen.

On Monday it was back to work. We moved *Astral Express* around to the fuel dock and Niclas helped me refuel. During the first part of the voyage the amount of fuel had been more critical as I had had to have enough for the full non-stop circumnavigation which was expected to be about six months. As I've mentioned earlier, when I left the boat in Greenland the tanks were nearly half full, so I would have had plenty without refilling. Now, though, with the balance of 10,000 miles to Auckland from Nuuk, I required less fuel and with full tanks again I had plenty in reserve for this last leg. As it turned out, I didn't refuel again until March 2011.

The following day Edward suggested we take her out of the water and give her a clean underneath. That evening we moved to a convenient wharf where his crane was waiting. Several people helped us attach slings to her and she was lifted out. A Nuuk Transport truck was on hand with water-blasting equipment, and soon *Astral Express* was looking new again.

A note about insurance: this was a matter for discussion, given that the boat no longer belonged to me and I was risking Edward's property rather than my own. There wasn't an insurance company in the world that would insure a boat going solo through the Northwest Passage. I got a letter of undertaking written up by my solicitor that I would cover any mishap. The insurance would kick back in once I'd got back down to around 45 degrees north.

Finally, Thursday rolled around. I motored slowly away from the wharf area to cheers, waves and best wishes. Soon she was under sail again and heading back up the fjord to join where I had left off on my outward journey. Niclas accompanied me for a few miles, circling in Edward's power boat, each of us taking photos.

I opened up the log book again and began my first entry with block letters: THANKS EDWARD!

19

INTO THE
ARCTIC CIRCLE

And now there came both mist and snow,
And it grew wondrous cold:
And ice, mast-high, came floating by,
As green as emerald.

And through the drifts the snowy clifts
Did send a dismal sheen:
Nor shapes of men nor beasts we ken—
The ice was all between.

—Samuel Coleridge, "The Rime of the Ancient Mariner"

I sailed out of the fjord and into Baffin Bay, heading north on a brilliant day, warm for this part of the world in late August. The weather forecast was good for the immediate area with a SSE 10–15 knots, increasing and turning SW. It was looking good. *Looks good, feels good, let's see.* I watched seals and birds working together, catching fish, the seals fast underwater, breaking the surface, and the birds swift in the air, plunging and rising. Stocky little brown and white birds swam and dived in the water – Little Auks, miles from land. They breed up here in the Arctic, but would soon migrate a little further south for the winter. There were hundreds of them across the surface of the water, and I sailed past them for several days.

Greenland's mountains receded as I made a steady seven knots through the start of Baffin Bay and into the Arctic Circle. I was a little further east and closer to the Greenland coast this time as I made my approach toward Lancaster Sound. Icebergs were ever-present but there were fewer of them over here on the east, which was encouraging.

After seven days sailing I had Lancaster Sound about 450 miles ahead at 74° north. There was ice forecast ahead and to the west but it was not blocking Lancaster Sound. At night I watched the Aurora Borealis dancing in the sky, a kaleidoscope of greens and blues.

I was feeling good. Positive. My nervousness had gone and I couldn't wait to get to Lancaster Sound, the destination that had eluded me last time.

Next morning dawned foggy. In the Arctic summer it was dark for only about two hours around midnight. Although the hours of darkness were increasing day by day, I was compensating by sailing ever-further north. By three in the morning it was full daylight, but the world was grey and visibility was very low. I had entered the sea ice but was trying to find my way around it to the west where I believed a lead was open enough for me to get up to Lancaster without going a long way around to the east.

It was cold, and I was well dressed in my new puffer jacket and waterproof trousers and three layers of thermal undergarments. I was well supplied with good clothing. I had my balaclava, gloves and beanie and goggles to wear in snow, sleet or rain, as well as my plastic imitation-fur-lined boots. I had two pairs of everything. I wouldn't have cut it on the ski field but I was warm enough for the Arctic Circle. I had two puffer jackets, this one I was wearing outside and a lighter weight one for inside, staying well dressed inside in preference to using the heaters.

It was that morning that, as I recounted in the Prologue to this book, I nearly came to grief by getting stuck in the ice. Baffin Bay has severe tides of four to nine metres, and this movement and volume puts enormous pressure on the fields of floating ice, crushing new and old ice into ragged forms. With my bow wedged between two three-metre blocks of ice I came face to face with what could be waiting for me – a winter in which I was unable to budge as the perpetual dark and the ice gathered and groaned around me. It was a terrifying thought and I worked like fury to get myself out of there. Imagine coming this far only to get stuck before even reaching Lancaster Sound.

With my heart in my mouth, which had gone unusually dry, I proceeded to extricate myself from this icy predicament. I managed to push *Astral Express* away from the ice using a pole which I carried for such an event. I began pushing the boat from the icy wedge and slowly managed to push free and turn it towards the direction I'd come from. The water was crystal clear and calm and I could see the submerged ice that the keel was hitting, Luckily, after a very stressful hour, I managed to turn the boat fully around even though it was still touching the ice underneath with the keel. From there I was able to sail back very slowly the way I'd come.

I was lucky the wind was so light and the ice hadn't moved about much, and within a few hours I reached moderately clear water. From there I sailed out to the east, taking the longer way round, then up north and back around to Lancaster Sound.

In that episode I really confronted the grim realities of this landscape. I learned my lesson. The relief was extraordinary, and all I could do was swallow one can of beer, and then another, scarcely tasting them.

Later that day I sailed past a pod of narwhals, lolling about near the surface, their heads bobbing above the waves. Narwhals get their name from the Old Norse word for "corpse" because their mottled greyish skin is like that of a drowned sailor. The males are very distinctive, and their single tusks appear speared out of the water, like needles, up to as much as three metres long. They're a very strange creature and I was glad to see them. Like all whales they've been severely hunted for meat and also for ivory.

Lancaster Sound is the body of water forming the eastern entrance to the Northwest Passage. It lies between the barren, rocky slopes of Devon and Baffin Islands, and I could see them both, each about 20 miles distant. Devon Island is the chosen site for the Flashline Mars Arctic Research Station, which since 2000 has been working towards preparing astronauts and scientists for life on Mars. It's a polar desert, dry and as cold as minus 50 degrees Celsius – the place on earth most like the environment found on Mars.

A few icebergs lay around the sound. I had worried there would be lots of them, but generally I had only one or two in sight at any one time. They are beautiful – they reach into the air 20–40 metres, in incredible shapes, but they are full of danger with their treacherous bulk beneath the water.

I had the radar tuned to a half-mile range, which meant the sea ice was showing up well. If it was big enough to do damage, I'd see it first. I had learned my lesson about the influence of the wind on ice. And I had discovered, almost to my peril, that ice charts were a guide, not a gospel. The vigilance required when sailing solo in this part of the world meant I had been sleeping no more than two hours at a time, often just snatching a few minutes.

It was just over a week since I'd left Nuuk as I sailed into Lancaster Sound, 360 miles north of the Arctic Circle. Once again it was early morning but full daylight. The previous month the sun hadn't set at all. It was still never far away, just dipping below the horizon, its loom visible even during the two hours from sunset to sunrise. With the Northern Lights dancing in the sky it made for an impressive display.

But now the early-morning fog had cleared, burned off by bright sunshine, and the world had turned to blue: blue sky, blue sea. I had a favourable current – which was why I'd chosen this east-to-west attempt – and *Astral Express* was sailing at an easy six or seven knots. Movement in the water caught my eye and a pod of about 30 beautiful, pure white beluga whales began swimming slowly with the boat.

What a day, what a welcome. Lancaster Sound was treating me kindly. My spirits lifted and I thought, *I've made it.*

ROUTE TAKEN BY *ASTRAL EXPRESS* THROUGH THE NORTHWEST PASSAGE

BEAUFORT SEA

BANKS IS.

Amundsen Gulf

NORTHWES

ALASKA

CAN

DEVON IS.

BAFFIN BAY

RESOLUTE
Barrow Strait

Lancaster Sound

SOMERSET
IS.

Peel Sound

PRINCE
OF
WALES
IS.

McClintock Channel

ORIA IS.

Franklin Strait

Admiralty Inlet

BAFFIN IS.

Cambridge
Bay

Meeting
with
Mathieu

KING
WILLIAM
IS.

*Queen
Maud Gulf*

ERRITORIE

A

20

OPEN WATER AMONG THE ICE SHEETS

To date, fewer people have sailed through the Northwest Passage than have reached the summit of Mount Everest.
—BBC News, 23 July 2014

The Northwest Passage snakes through a maze of islands and a tangle of channels, many of them iced up. From Lancaster Sound to the western tip of Alaska at Barrow Point, the passage stretches for a total distance of about 1850 nautical miles. No wonder it was so hard for early explorers to find a way through – and the way is only open for exploration for a matter of weeks each year.

I was now in communication with Peter Semotiuk, the radio operator who lived in Cambridge Bay, a small settlement in the middle part of the Northwest Passage, and he was giving me encouraging reports of conditions ahead. He was also guiding some other vessels approaching from the west.

Canadian ice reports showed extensive ice ahead blocking Prince Regent Inlet, which is the normal or preferred route. However, behind the ice sheet, Peel Sound, the next opportunity to go south, looked clear.

By early morning on 28 August fog had set in and ice was starting to appear ahead. The charts showed it was clear to the north up towards the town of Resolute, but that was quite a long way off the ideal course. On the southern edge there appeared to be a clearer channel or gap in the ice close to shore. I decided to go for this and by midday I was in the thick of it. Fog was lifting slightly. It was a grey day but at least it wasn't raining. Dressed for the conditions, I attempted to sail through what looked on the charts to be a clear channel but turned out not to be quite so. It was navigable but not in a straight line and it required continuous steering and meandering through the treacherous area. Ice to port was solid all the way to the shore.

It was slow going but by mid-afternoon I had made a few miles in the right direction. I'd made several hits against pieces that I couldn't avoid and which were small, about the size of a table and 80 per cent submerged. When I hit them they went under the bow, hit the steel keel and usually split in two and popped up each side at the back. There would be a lot of pieces of ice this year with blue anti-fouling paint on them.

The boat had been designed with a lifting keel for just these conditions. When I was in the ocean I had it down to its full extent for better performance. The stability of the deep keel was what got me through Hurricane Harvey. But here in the Passage I lifted it so I could go through shallow water and also because with the keel up, which took it from dropping two metres to just one, the lead bulb would protect the rudder and the propeller if I hit ice. I could now see that this plan was working perfectly – so far, anyway.

I was certain that if conditions didn't get any worse I would be able to get through this area. The chart showed the ice extending for a further 50 miles so I needed to be absolutely on alert. It's in these conditions that the cost of sailing alone becomes apparent – there's no-one to take a watch and I would just have to stay awake.

I couldn't leave the helm, and with ice on deck and the wind gear at the top of the mast already frozen, I needed to be careful. It was thermos coffee and soup all the way, and by midnight I was getting really tired, but I could see on the chart that there was clear water about 10 miles ahead. By 7am I'd been up for more than 24 hours and had sailed 200 miles into Lancaster Sound. The entrance to Peel Sound was about 30 miles ahead. There I could turn south. With binoculars I could see that the way ahead towards Peel Sound was now clear of ice.

I put the autopilot on, set a waypoint alarm on the chart plotter, and with the radar alarm also set I headed down for two hours of sleep.

Refreshed, I breakfasted on coffee and muesli and enjoyed the fine morning as I entered Peel Sound, with Somerset Island to port and Prince of Wales Island to starboard, making my way south to Franklin Strait, about 200 miles distant. Ice reports showed this to be mainly ice-free and it looked like a possible shortcut through Victoria Strait, which was seldom navigable. This would save about 140 miles and prevent having to sail to the east around King William Island and Gjoa Haven, the only settlement on King William Island and the harbour where Amundsen spent two years iced in before successfully navigating the Passage in 1906.

The land and mountains of Peel Sound are brown and barren in the sunlight, dark and looming when the light is dim or when cloud comes down. And the distances in this part of the world are vast.

When you look at a map of the world, the Arctic waterways and islands appear very small and compact. The Northwest Passage seems to crowd narrowly above Canada. But while there are parts that are close, generally it's very open, providing it's not iced over. If you're going up the centre of a sound you can usually see land on either side but it could be several miles away.

Some areas are indeed very narrow, though. For instance, Bellot Strait which separates the southern tip of Somerset Island from the Boothia Peninsula is used by a lot of boats, and it's tight, only about a half mile wide. I wasn't keen to go that way, and as it turned out it was iced over, which was unusual. As I came down Peel Sound, Bellot Strait came up on my port side; the area around its entrance was iced so I kept well to the west of it.

Now that I was in the Passage, I thought: *Well, I'm committed.* The further I went, the more committed I was. I had to keep going to get out the other side, and every mile I did was one more behind me. That was a good feeling.

It was fairly demanding sailing from the point of view of navigation. It was all about making choices. I got information from the charts – and I hoped they were accurate – and I decided which way I was going to go. But the decisions were often based on uncertainty.

However, I was lucky. The weather was good and I had favourable wind, and that was a help. If I'd gone through when it was stormy it could have been a very different experience. Having to manage the boat in a storm at the same time as looking out for ice wouldn't have been easy, and I knew I was fortunate. A few days after me in certain areas, the weather did pack in – the wind changed, the ice gathered and at least one person had to be rescued.

But for now I was lucky and I sailed on.

The northerly breeze freshened astern and I reduced sail, reefing in the main headsails furled and running dead downwind. Perfect. I was sitting on about eight knots and keeping to the middle of the 15-mile wide strait.

There were many small islands near the shore and a few icebergs, but these appeared less frequently as I proceeded south. There was also wildlife about, with seals, whales, the ever-present birds and polar bears foraging on the distant shore. I watched the polar bears through the binoculars and saw they were discoloured from being on dry land. The closest I came to them was about 300 metres. One or two looked in my direction and I knew they knew I was there. What aromas were they getting? I was too far away, though, and sailing faster than they could swim. They just went about their business.

The wind was now about 20 knots so I was looking at a good day's run.

I was communicating regularly with Peter Semotiuk of Cambridge Bay. He called to inform me of a Frenchman, Mathieu Bonnier, who was trying to row part of the Northwest Passage. Peter thought I might be getting pretty close to him, and said I should look out for him as he may need some assistance or a rest. I didn't think too much of it. He was doing his thing and I was doing mine. If I saw him and he needed help then I would assist, of course.

The weak afternoon sun soon cleared the ice off the deck and my happy hour rum tasted really good that evening.

ABOVE: The icebox kept so cold in the cockpit I was able to carry fresh meat for the first five weeks.

BELOW: Bottlenose whales follow me through Davis Strait.

ABOVE: Northwest Passage fashion: dressed for the occasion.

BELOW: Icebergs were ever-present as I sailed into the Arctic Circle, approaching the Northwest Passage.

ABOVE: Clear waters in the Northwest Passage.

BELOW: Now laquered interior, featuring the blue leather navigation chair.

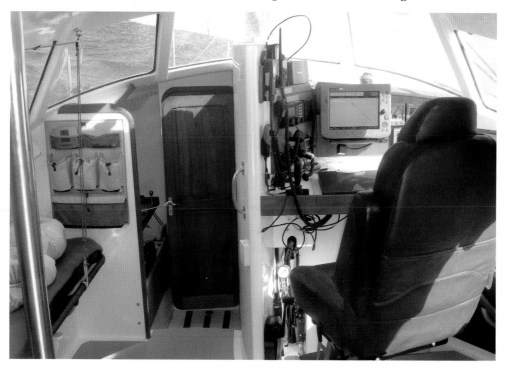

ABOVE: Matthieu Bonnier and his dog Tico, about to come aboard *Astral Express*. I had just thrown him a line.

BELOW: Ice like this is only just navigable in the Northwest Passage.

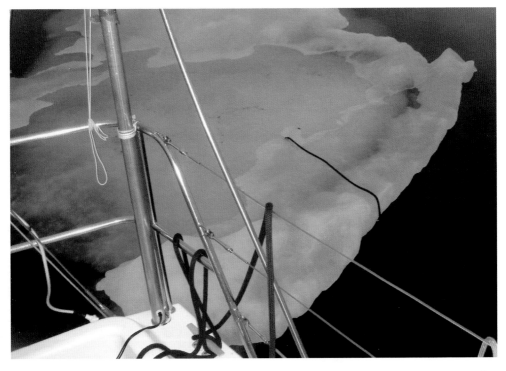

ABOVE: Anchored to ice at the beginning of Dease Strait – one way to get a good night's sleep, if there aren't any polar bears around.

BELOW: Seas starting to build up in the Bering Sea. [ISTOCKPHOTO.COM]

ABOVE: A resounding crash: this is the small iceberg I hit and glanced off as I sailed through Victoria Strait.

BELOW: My course through Dease Straight as seen on the GPS screen.

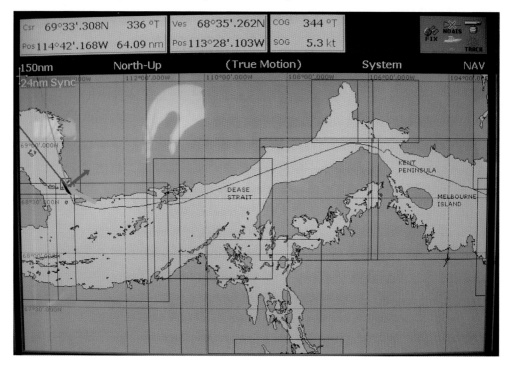

Csr 69°33'.308N   336 °T   Ves 68°35'.262N   COG   344 °T
Pos 114°42'.168W   64.09 nm   Pos 113°28'.103W   SOG   5.3 kt

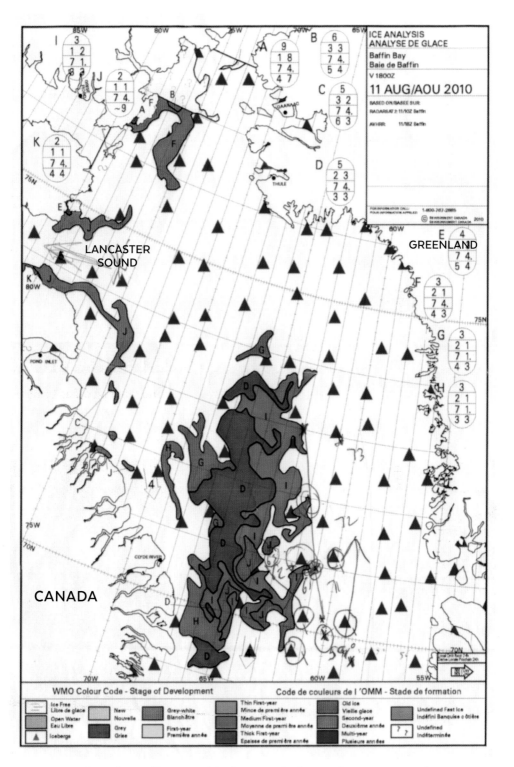

Ice chart for Baffin Bay with the many icebergs shown as triangles.

ABOVE: Arriving home in Auckland Harbour.

LEFT: Franceska, flowers, family and friends. [IVOR WILKINS]

BELOW LEFT: Champagne, the taste of home. [IVOR WILKINS]

BELOW: Thanks Edward Niclasen. [IVOR WILKINS]

21

COMPANY FOR DINNER

Graeme was probably thinking I was crazy, and I was thinking he was crazy.

To have dinner, a glass of wine, in such a place on the planet was more than strange. It was a fantastic welcome.

Graeme is very cool – he controls the situation but he was tired with sleep deprivation. With this ice in these narrow passages he could not sleep for 10 minutes. It was very stressful to manage during the night. But he was going very, very fast. Crazy fast. I'm sure no-one can beat his crossing for a very long time.

—Mathieu Bonnier

Next morning I entered Franklin Strait with the usual morning fog smothering the edges of everything in grey. But luckily it wasn't a pea soup, so I could keep my look out for ice. The fog is usually gone by noon.

I got another call from Peter with an update on Mathieu Bonnier. The Frenchman was very tired and lonely and he had had about enough. Within the hour I received a phone call from Mathieu himself, who was anxious to give me his position. I told him I was about 45 miles away and should be able to see him if I veered a little to port as I got close to Victoria Strait. After another anxious call from Mathieu within a few hours, I told him I was on course to see him, and he reiterated his position.

I had now sailed about 1490 miles since leaving Nuuk and it was 30 August. By evening the wind had eased and I was using the binoculars, on lookout for Mathieu. His position was just off the northern tip of King William Island and it looked as if he also was contemplating the shortcut through Victoria Strait.

Franklin Sound is, of course, named for Captain John Franklin, who led the ill-famed expedition of two ships, HMS *Erebus* and HMS *Terror*, in search of the Northwest Passage in 1845. The ships never returned, and nor did any of the 129 crew. For many years it was a mystery, and it was only in the late 20th century that their fates began to be pieced together. Finally, in 2014 the underwater archaeologist Ryan Harris found the wreck of the *Erebus* where Franklin Strait converges with Victoria Strait – exactly beneath the spot that I was now about to rendezvous with Matheiu Bonnier.

We now know that the ships became ice-bound here at the northwest tip of King William Island, having sailed down Peel Strait and Franklin Strait as I myself was now doing, but with worse luck. They came into what anthropologist Owen Beattie described as a "ploughing train of ice" that failed to melt in the summer, and there they were stranded for two years, the ships eventually becoming crushed. Meanwhile, the surviving crew attempted to haul themselves to safety over the remote terrain of King William Island, all eventually dying in the attempt – of scurvy, lead poisoning and starvation. There was even cannibalism. Nothing illustrates the harsh danger of this environment more clearly than the fate of the Franklin expedition.

But on this evening, as I sighted Mathieu over the silky blue water of the sound, all was calm and neither of us was aware of the wreck lying beneath us.

I saw him from a distance – a small, purpose-built rowing boat, and the tall figures of a man and his dog, an Alaskan Malamute. The wind was light and with just the mainsail up I manoeuvred *Astral Express* alongside the small craft.

With fenders in place I took a line and assisted him aboard. The beautiful dog – Tico, after whom Mathieu's expedition was named – was left aboard his boat and we let the line out so I could keep it in tow as I sailed on at a slow pace. Mathieu was a little shaken as I welcomed him on board and sat him down inside. We each explained our reasons for being there, and developed an immediate mutual respect.

In 2009 he had rowed across the Atlantic. Now it was his goal to row the Northwest Passage, taking two seasons to do it – with the limited window of opportunity it would not be possible to row the whole way in one year. He had set out from Qaanaaq on Greenland's north coast and had become the first person to row from Greenland to Canada, a distance of 230 nautical miles that took him 12 days.

But he'd been having a real struggle with wind. Rowing and wind close to the shore is not a good mix, and one day he'd had to battle against 47 knots of wind with a lot of ice. He was cold and exhausted. To top it off, he had seen a lot of polar bears.

I had two steaks left in the chilly bin. I suggested he stay for dinner, and he gladly accepted. I also had a small cask of red wine and I poured him some in my only glass. We toasted each other, me drinking from a cup.

He was very tired, so after dinner he lay down for an hour or so, and then I offered him coffee which he refused until he saw me making plunger coffee for myself. "Oh, I'll have one of those," he said. He couldn't believe it, and in later communications referred to *Astral Express* as the "Franklin Strait restaurant". He thought I was very well set up. He had brought his camera on board and took photos of us and gave me a pack of cheese that he said he would no longer require. It was a fine gift – gourmet cheese, purchased in France.

We discussed the possibility of taking a shortcut through Victoria Strait. We had both realised that as the ice wasn't too bad in there it was a way of cutting 140 miles off the trip. This channel is 170 miles long and about 70 miles wide, making it one of the largest channels in this area, but it's usually ice-blocked all year because it lies open to the McClintock Channel which feeds Arctic ice into this area, especially when the prevailing northerly winds are strong. With the Canadian mainland to the south and the series of islands above, a maze of channels and straits is formed but is usually all iced up. No wonder early explorers found it hard to find a northwest passage.

After a few hours I sailed as close as I could to the coast of King William Island and we said goodbye. He rowed ashore – he was doing this every day to give his dog a run around. It was a most congenial meeting.

I sailed on, the shortcut working well for me. But unfortunately for Mathieu the weather packed in behind me and he copped some very stormy weather, and the ice came in. As it happened, the television adventurer Bear Grylls was travelling the Northwest Passage by motor boat at the same time, followed by a very big yacht with a big engine and plenty of luxurious equipment. He invited Mathieu aboard, but Mathieu turned him down – although he eventually asked them to rescue his dog and take it with them to Cambridge Bay.

He was experiencing increasingly bad weather. A nasty storm blew up and he described being pushed around by a piece of ice as big as a house.

At its worst, the wind was 60 knots. The coastguard was unable to reach him, and so he had to stay in his boat until the weather finally calmed. He was well equipped and wore a dry suit so that even when he fell in the water his body was dry. He had emergency equipment and knew he could escape on to the ice, but he didn't want to abandon his boat.

Mathieu didn't end up completing the passage. He realised it wasn't possible to do it in two years, and he wasn't prepared to commit to the several years it actually required. He ended up selling his rowing boat to a man who also wanted to row the Northwest Passage. This man began from the west side. He is currently into his third year and is close to Cambridge Bay, so still with a long way to go.

I was more fortunate, however. As I sailed through, Victoria Strait had around two-tenths ice coverage which, with careful navigation, was manageable. With daylight hours and a light wind, I was able to make my way south towards Queen Maud Gulf, where I would turn west.

It was rewarding to sail through this area as few vessels had ever done it, and it was good to know I was saving about 140 miles. Reports were coming in that a fuel tanker had gone aground over on the east side of King William Island, so I was doubly pleased I'd chosen this way.

Clear ahead, calm sea, light wind, sailing at five knots. There was open water between ice sheets now and with a clear forecast ahead it was time for a quick rest.

I lay down and had soon gone to sleep.

Wham.

There was a resounding crash and the boat came to a complete stop. My legs folded against the bulkhead as I woke. It took a few seconds to focus as I sat up with my heart in my mouth. Rushing up on deck I saw a scraggy small iceberg blocking the way, the size of a truck above the water. I had moved it slightly with the crash. I inspected the bow for damage. There was nothing to be seen, and with sails still up *Astral Express* drifted off to port and we sailed on in clear water.

It took a few hours to get over the shock of this. I had been too complacent with the ice charts, I admonished myself. And being tired I hadn't set the alarms.

When I was just about through Victoria Strait, I was briefly becalmed – a tiny yacht floating on a glass surface among reflected clouds. But then a few ripples disturbed the surface as a SE wind arrived and my course changed to the west to sail across Queen Maud Gulf towards the entrance to Dease Strait. I was getting close to Cambridge Bay, the small settlement where Peter Semotiuk lives and where most boats stop.

22

AGROUND

*Late in the night I woke, feeling restless and uneasy. There was
something unusual in the movement of the waves . . . I could get no
quiet sleep. Time passed.*
—Thor Heyerdahl, Kon Tiki: Across the Pacific by Raft

With the wind freshening in the afternoon I set the alarms to take a nap.

I woke with my heart in my mouth, another tremendous bang echoing
through the boat from below. Bells were ringing. What the hell! Waking
up with a sound like that is horrific. You hear this noise and you don't
know if you're dreaming it or if it's actually happened.

What could it be? I knew there was no ice in the area. I must have run
aground. Again I rushed on deck to survey the situation. Sure enough
– hard aground.

I immediately dropped all sails and walked around the deck looking down to see what I had run aground on. The water was crystal clear, about two metres deep, but I could see that I had run aground on a boulder bank, the boulders small, smooth and slippery with lichen. The incredible noise came from the lead bulb on the bottom keel grinding over these rocks.

I was acutely aware of how remote I was out there. This was potentially a dire situation.

Increasing my difficulty was that because I'd already been sailing with the keel up, I didn't have the option of raising it to float off the rocks.

In ordinary life there's always someone to call in an emergency – a friend, a doctor, a policeman. Something, someone.

Not here.

I did have a credit card with me, my thinking being that if I needed to call for a helicopter in a disaster I could, although where that was going to come from, who knows. Under that scenario I would have to abandon the boat and maybe go back next season to see if it was still there. That was such an awful scenario I could scarcely even consider it.

If I got iced in and stayed, the practicalities of trying to live for six months in the dark, with everything frozen up around me, were not attractive. I would soon run out of battery power, although I could run the engine occasionally. But the toilet wouldn't work. And there would be no certainty that when summer rolled around I could get off. Ice doesn't always melt from one year to another, and I'd still be grounded.

Far better to solve this problem. *Think it through!* After checking the depth again, I could see that the shoal seemed to fall away on the starboard side. With the wind coming from the port side, the headsail might swing the boat to starboard and off this shoal.

Also, I could raise the keel a few more centimetres if I could remove the huge stainless steel pin that usually held it up. So I did this using the hydraulic pump, then quickly unfurled the headsail, sheeting it in tight as Astral Express turned in the desired direction and began to move. As

I eased the headsail she picked up speed and the keel moved clear. Then *crunch* again. Lifting the keel that far meant the rudder was hanging down below the keel and now it was hitting the rocks.

But with a few bumps the rudder popped the pin holding it in its casing and slid up about 200 millimetres. We were free and off. Phew!

I didn't need any more of these shocks.

I got the sails up again, and I carried on, jittery with relief.

Afterwards people asked me why I didn't use the motor. It was always there as an option – it wasn't like a yacht race where you couldn't use it. But I preferred not to use it if I didn't need to. Partly it was a point of pride.

And in this instance I knew that I'd turn the boat faster by putting the headsail up. The headsail was like having a motor in the front. It turned the boat, twisted it on the keel and then moved it forward.

The shoal was on the charts but it might have been slightly bigger than when it was mapped, or the charts could have been off. Although they're quite accurate they can be out a few metres or a few hundred metres. It means you can't rely on GPS and have to be vigilant with radar and sight.

It was a huge relief to be able to spin the boat and sail out. But I was feeling pretty spooked. I was a bit sleep-deprived, but these near misses exacerbated the feeling I had about this part of the world – I had no desire to hang around here. It felt like a hot potato. *Let's get the hell out of here.* I had that feeling all the time. *Keep moving.*

I had the feeling that I was in – not forbidden territory exactly – but an area of the world that really wasn't designed for humans. Not for me, anyway. It's inhospitable. I know people do live there – they fish, live off the land, dress for the weather. But I suppose I'm expressing my personal response to its remoteness and its harshness.

I was on my own. I had been on my own for months when I sailed from Auckland up to this region and it hadn't bothered me, nor struck me particularly. But up here I felt it. I was totally on my own.

If I can't do it myself, no-one else is going to do it for me.

———

With about 100 miles to sail across Queen Maud Gulf to Dease Strait entrance I was on lookout as ice was ever present, and not long after sunrise I saw a large ice field ahead. This hadn't been forecast and must have drifted down from McClintock Channel and Icebreaker Channel. The day was clear and the morning fog lifting, so it couldn't have been better timing as I tried to sail through on a direct course to Dease Strait.

With calm water and light wind it was actually quite picturesque. I watched myself sail by as the shadow of the yacht played on the ice I was sliding past. I enjoyed the peace, and relaxed with a cup of soup. But it was soon apparent there was no way through. So I headed back the way I'd come in and proceeded south around the ice edge. It took a full day's sailing, making my way around the ice sheet in Queen Maud Sound. The ice was closer than it appeared and it flattened the sea. The fog and ice seemed to go together.

By midnight I had finally arrived close to the entrance of Dease Strait, totally becalmed and drifting with pack ice. There was no point trying to sail and I was really tired, so I dropped the sail thinking I'd just drift along for a bit. It was quite a safe area. The ice was just flat pieces.

At that point I noticed that *Astral Express* was drifting faster than the ice – perhaps I was catching a bit of current underneath. It was marginal, but I was desperate for sleep and I thought that if I was going to shut my eyes I wanted to drift as little as possible.

So with the wind completely gone I tied a rope to the ice axe and used it to moor the boat to a large piece of ice. Now I was only drifting slowly and it was time to get a few hours' sleep before the sun came up. It was rather broken sleep, with ice scraping along the hull at times in this congested area. I was also slightly alert for white visitors; I slept with the door partly closed in case of polar bears, although I'd heard from the Alaskan forecasters that polar bears can break down any door on a ship. I could shoot through a small hatch . . . but luckily it was not required this night.

What a difference daylight and a good sleep makes. I woke at five or six in the morning, had coffee and food, and felt rejuvenated. I remembered something I'd written on my blog during the first trip: "Some days are good, others excellent. The excellent ones usually come after a good night's sleep."

I had drifted about a quarter mile in the right direction during the night. I retrieved the axe, poled away from the ice, and got back underway. The channel was easy to see about two miles ahead with only a few patches of ice visible. Sailing through these and turning SW I could see down Dease Strait and it looked ice-free. Great!

Dease Strait is about 100 miles long. Cambridge Bay, from where Peter Semotiuk broadcasts, was up on the northern side of the strait, on the southern tip of Victoria Island, probably around ten miles away, but I didn't sail past and wave. Dease eventually opens out and becomes Coronation Gulf, then turns northwest with a narrow channel bordering small islands that leads into Dolphin and Union Strait. It's an area that needs careful navigation.

My previous day's run had been only 106 miles, but now with clear water and a favourable wind I began to make good progress through this barren land. The low hills either side had no trees and were rocky and covered at this time of year with lichen and short grasses. For most of the year they are snow covered, and always in permafrost at this latitude, which is still 70° north. I was anxious to be out of this place.

Again I had that feeling: *The ice belongs here, I don't.*

The satellite ice charts showed this area to be clear of ice, and so far they had been accurate. Conditions were a bit different here from earlier sections of the passage, as there are no straits coming down from the north, meaning no ice can be blown down into these waters.

My daily mileage crept up to 125 and 135 miles. I settled into my normal daily routine and enjoyed the weak summer sun in my cockpit. Just across Coronation Gulf I passed a crewed yacht, a Finnish steel ketch, heading for the town of Kugluktuk, on the southwest tip of Victoria Island.

For all its remoteness, a number of tourist boats go through here each year. You can buy a ticket and go on a passenger boat through the Northwest Passage. They're usually big enough to be able to smash through ice. They'll carry a helicopter that can fly up and get a good view and tell them which way to go to avoid ice.

Back in 1994 the former United States Secretary of the Treasury Bill Simon did the passage on his yacht *Itasca*. He went from east to west and achieved the first single-season eastbound traverse of the Northwest Passage by a private yacht – he did it in just over 23 days. But his was a very different project to mine. He went through powered by two 1250 hp engines, his interior fitted out in considerable luxury, and with a crew of about 10 high-powered specialists.

I was pleased to be doing this my way – solo, under sail – and more than happy with my relatively spartan but highly functional decor. With this progress and a good ice forecast ahead for the northern coast of Alaska, I started to feel that I had a good chance of accomplishing the transit of this fabled passage.

Anyway, it was starting to look as if I might create a record or two of my own. No-one, as far as I knew, had previously sailed this route by themselves.

And, as it turned out, no-one had gone through as fast as I was.

23

TO THE GRIM WEST

As if the Sea should part
And show a further Sea —
And that — a further — and the Three
But a presumption be —
Of Periods of Seas —
Unvisited of Shores —
Themselves the Verge of Seas to be —
Eternity — is Those —
—Emily Dickinson, "As if the Sea should part"

Ice was moving in behind me. I got a call from Peter Semotiuk on 4 September to say that Mathieu had been rescued – he was tired and had badly blistered hands but was okay. After I'd left the Victoria Sound area a moderate northwest gale had come in and filled it with ice. He just couldn't row through. Soon after I got a call from Mathieu himself, and I congratulated him on his fine effort nevertheless.

Joel called the same day. I was in regular contact with him as he was doing my weather for me, but this time it was different.

"Just letting you know we've had an earthquake," he said. "But everything's okay."

That was as much as I knew. But he'd said everything was okay, so I didn't think it was a big issue – until I found out later it was really big. That was the first of the Christchurch earthquakes that laid waste to the city and the surrounding region – 7.1 on the Richter scale.

Of course, once I got back home there were further earthquakes in February and the following June. It was so sad. I thought of my parents and how they wouldn't be able to believe all the changes to their home town. All those families with homes and businesses and assets – the earthquakes changed the values and the timeframe of all their plans.

I was pleased that family and friends were all safe, although that first one was just the precursor. The third one dropped one of the family homes completely.

But for now, with that first earthquake, I was a long way away and there was nothing I could do. In fact on that day I was a bit more relaxed and feeling pretty good.

Coming up to the Amundsen Gulf I had fine weather and calm seas and was able to get jobs done around the boat. She was spic and span and I congratulated myself and everyone who had been involved with her design and construction. What a great vessel!

I aired my clothes and got some good sleep and felt I was getting back into a daily routine.

A note about sleep. Because of the way I had my cabin laid out, it was possible for me to lie on my bunk, my head aft and my feet pointing forward, and check everything by just opening my eyes. The windows were angled so I could see the mainsail, the headsail and the wind indicator on the top of the mast. I could look across at the instruments, and I could hear that the boat was doing exactly what it was doing when I set it up. If the wind had changed I would hear it. In fact, so finely tuned was I to the boat that I would wake if there was the slightest change. If I was lying down I would put the radar on. If the autopilot should get off course, the alarm would go for that too.

By this stage of the trip I was used to getting whatever I could in the way of sleep. An hour or two was enough to keep me going for another three or four hours. If I knew the way was clear for the next 20 miles, and I was doing four or five knots, then I knew I had four or five hours.

Probably my longest sleep through the Northwest Passage was the five or six hours I got out on the Beaufort Sea. Mostly I wasn't getting that much – it was more likely to be three or four hours. But a three or four-hour sleep with a half hour up then another three or four seemed to work fine.

Sometimes during the day I'd catnap, or just sit out in cockpit if there was a bit of sun. I learned to rest. I had a very nice leather helm seat inside and I could stand behind that and hang my hands over it, knowing I could do that for only five minutes, but sometimes that was enough to be able to carry on. But by the time I was in the Northwest Passage I was conditioned to sleeping in short bursts, and I managed it fairly easily.

I had many indelible experiences during my circumnavigation, but one of my favourites was waking unexpectedly into the full throes of the Aurora Borealis (otherwise known as the Northern Lights, a psychodelic display in the sky caused by charged particles from the sun reacting with the magnetic field in the Arctic). I was lying on my bunk, but looking up through my cabin windows I could see green lights dancing through the sky and I wondered at first if I was dreaming.

Of course, I often saw it when I was outside, but this was so unexpected. From where I lay I checked the top of my mast, the headsail, the instruments, and then I lay there watching that incredible display.

I had a good couple of days' run through the 250 miles of the Amundsen Gulf. With more open water now the sea had become lumpy again and I sailed in light rain for the first time in a while. With deep water now all the way ahead I put the keel down. It had been up since 26 August and done good work deflecting lots of ice while protecting the folding prop and rudder.

My compass had been useless ever since Peel Sound, unable to function that close to the magnetic North Pole. Now it was working again, but it was a moot point. I hadn't used it at all so far, having always used paper charts to survey the way ahead. Providing I was moving, the satellite GPS positioning system showed my course on the chart plotter screen.

Rain washed the salt off *Astral Express* as I entered the grim Beaufort Sea. Part of the Arctic Ocean, it's frozen most of the year but at this time of year there was a corridor of water between the northern Canadian and Alaskan coast and the ice edge, which was about 10 miles north. From there, the frozen Arctic extended all the way to the North Pole.

Close to shore are oil wells and pingos, huge earth-covered ice mounds. There are around 1350 of these in this region, including eight protected ones in the area around Tuktoyaktuk, a tiny hamlet on the shore of the Beaufort Sea.

As I pushed out into the ocean, heading for Point Barrow, the official end of the Northwest Passage some 1280 kilometres, or 650 nautical miles, away, I felt what a barren area it was. I saw no birds at all, the first time on the entire trip I had been without my feathered companions. It was an area of the world I didn't want to be in too long. I was keen to get out of there.

I listened to Sarah Brightman's song "Sleep Tight" again and again – it was daunting but fitting for the environment. If you ever wanted visual images to accompany that song, the Beaufort Sea was a perfect match – grim, grey, threatening and bleak. The reaper at night. It was all so ominous it was almost amusing. I really felt my predicament, to be sailing north of Alaska with nothing in sight and not a hope of rescue.

It was cold. The wind and rain on the Beaufort Sea brought the temperature down and at night it was close to freezing. A couple of times at night it got really cold and the instruments on top of the mast froze and wouldn't operate. They thawed out quite quickly during the day. I tied cloth around the stainless steel hand holds inside because they also attracted the cold.

It was just above freezing, but it was bleak and damp and I wore wet-weather gear, gloves and so on. I continued to find it easier to dress up for the cold rather than use heating. The heater in the cabin wasn't very efficient, and I wasn't sure about the carbon dioxide of the heater, especially as I was on my own. I just thought that was something I could do without. I found that if I used a lightweight puffer jacket for inside and a thicker one for outside, I stayed warm that way. Once I was inside out of the wind, it felt warmer anyway.

It was too cold to change clothes much so I just keep it all on for a few days. I'd had the odd shower coming through the passage, but it was tempting not to bother when the weather got really cold. Baby wipes are good in those conditions – or just waiting for warmer weather.

With a fresh 20-knot easterly wind and a favourable current I started to increase my daily runs, with the best across being 180 miles. At least I was romping along in the right direction. I had Alaska below me to the south now. Ice was forecast to be congested in Prudhoe Bay at 71°40' north, so I took a wide berth around that area, tacking hard on the wind until I could take a clear run towards Point Barrow.

On Wednesday 8 September I reached Point Barrow, the exit point for the Northwest Passage. I was excited to be there, but unfortunately I arrived in pea-soup fog. The point was completely shrouded, even though I sailed as close as possible. From four miles away it only just showed up on radar as it is low lying. I could hear the radio station of the tiny settlement there – Alaska's northernmost settlement – but there was no chance of seeing it. Captain Cook's journals report that he had a similar experience a short way further south where he noted "a fog bank" that prevented him from seeing the land.

Nevertheless, I knew it was there.

I had sailed the Northwest Passage and it was time for double rum that night.

Lots of congratulations were coming in, including from Peter Semotiuk who confirmed I was the first solo sailor to successfully complete this passage non-stop.

In my log I listed my feelings: *Unique, privileged, remote, lonely, scared, proud, lucky, sensational, hard work.*

———

I recorded a total distance from Lancaster Sound to Barrow Point of 1782 miles at an average speed of 146 miles per day, the slowest being 106 miles as I went through Queen Maud Gulf, and the fastest being 180 miles when I was in the Beaufort Sea. The shortcut via Victoria Strait saved me about 146 miles, more than an average day's sailing.

I had estimated it would take about two weeks to sail the Northwest Passage, provided I had no major problems with ice and headwinds. To do it in a fast 12 days in a thoroughbred vessel didn't really surprise me. Most boats stop for provisioning, sightseeing and repairs, and I did it non-stop. As it turned out, sailing east to west provided favourable currents in the right direction and winds more so.

My feelings echoed those of Roald Amundsen on his completion of the Northwest Passage in 1905 as he encountered a ship coming from the West and knew he had made it through: "The North West Passage was done. My boyhood dream – at that moment it was accomplished. A strange feeling welled up in my throat; I was somewhat over-strained and worn – it was weakness in me – but I felt tears in my eyes. Vessel in sight . . . Vessel in sight."

AUTUMN HEADWINDS

There was a deafening screaming of birds over us all that night. And
the moon was nearly full.
—Thor Heyerdahl, *Kon Tiki: Across the Pacific by Raft*

I'd made it. I felt like getting off the boat. I wanted a good hotel and a
celebration. I wanted to see my family and friends. It was over.

But the grey waters slapped the boat and the fog pressed down, and
the wind pushed into the sails.

It wasn't over.

The Chukchi Sea, Bering Strait, Bering Sea and the full length of the
Pacific Ocean lay ahead before me.

Also, as I'd always known they would be, the adverse currents and contrary winds of the northern autumn were waiting to lay into me as soon as I turned south down the northwest coast of Alaska. And now the days were shortening, each one 12 minutes darker than the one before.

Tuning in to local Alaskan radio stations I heard an astonishing fact: the Alaskan Monarch butterfly migrates to Mexico in the winter and then returns to Alaska to breed in the summer, each butterfly only managing this incredible journey once in a lifespan of eight months. I have been constantly amazed during this long voyage at the patterns of nature. In cities we're largely divorced from it, but out on the oceans I was so aware of it: nature going about its business.

Sure enough, as I sailed past the town of Wainwright I ran into headwinds. It wouldn't have been so bad but I also had an adverse one-to-one-and-a-half-knot current running against me, so my daily runs slowed to only about 125 miles. I passed Icy Cape, 142 miles southwest of Point Barrow, a headland thrusting into the frigid Chukchi Sea. This was as far as Captain Cook came in 1778 in his attempt to chart Alaska and discover the Northwest Passage. He reached here on 17 August and then had to retreat because of an advancing ice field. His journal records his impression of the ice, the like of which he had not seen before: ". . . [I]t is evident that [the ice] now covered a part of the sea which but a few days before was clear and that it extended farther to the South than where we first fell in with it. It must not be understood that I supposed any part of the ice we had seen fixed, on the contrary I am well assured that the whole was a moveable Mass . . ."

Cook escaped by tacking through openings in the floes. The weather, he noted, was "very hazey with drizling rain". He "did not think it consistent with prudence to make any farther attempts to find a passage this year in any direction so little was the prospect of succeeding". He planned to return the following summer but it was not to be. He headed south to Hawaii and there he was killed.

Psychologically, for me, this was the hard part of the trip. I had achieved, yet I hadn't finished. I was starting to realise what the Northwest Passage had taken out of me. I was fatigued, physically and mentally, and I wanted a breather – but that was not on the cards.

I hadn't realised how the mental and emotional stress and strain had added up. There was something about being in that passage, knowing that in three or four weeks what I was doing would be impossible. That the ice was coming. That I didn't belong there. It all felt a bit surreal, and I was aware all the time of wanting to get out of there. *Keep moving. Keep moving.* There was danger and I thought that the prospect of dying was strange, but then not as strange as being born in the first place.

I'd given it 100 per cent. I felt tremendous satisfaction and relief on achieving it. But the self-congratulation faded quite quickly, because the job wasn't done yet. I still had more than 7000 miles to sail until I could hope to see New Zealand's long white cloud.

———

One good thing was that as I sailed further south, the birds came back. That made my spirits lift. It had been such an indelible part of the trip, this constant presence of birds, and I always looked for them. Where's the bird today? Oh, there it is – the black-hooded gull that breeds in the area, and also the Short-tailed Shearwater that breeds in Australia but comes all the way up here for the short northern summer.

Apart from that time in the Beaufort Sea there was never a day on the trip when there wasn't a bird about the boat. It was as if there was a bird carrying me on the journey. Not the same one, but always one there.

I suspect all sailors have a special feeling about birds, and it's especially strong when you're on your own. You feel you have a guardian angel, in a way. In the long hours of solitude I would sit in my cockpit and watch them and feel awed by them – by flight itself, by the way they live, their independence. I felt good watching them.

As I approached Point Hope the wind and seas rose, especially as the water was shallow here at only 18 metres. I worked my way through it for a few days, but it was hard to make progress. It was exhausting and I was getting nowhere. By the fourth week of September it had become a moderate SSE gale, so I decided it would be better to find shelter and let it subside.

By this stage I was approaching Bering Strait, where two islands sit about four miles apart – Little Diomede and Big Diomede. At this point, Russia and the United States face each other across just 55 miles of sea. Russia owns Big Diomede, and Little Diomede is part of the United States of America. In the winter the two are linked by frozen ice, meaning it's possible – although not legal – to walk from Russia to the United States.

Russia claimed Alaska in the 19th century but sold it to the United States in 1867, before gold and oil were discovered there. I keep wondering if the Russian who sold Alaska to the Americans had been sent to the salt mines. Interesting that the United Kingdom turned down the opportunity to buy Alaska. The United States also had second thoughts, but 20 years after its purchase they had made back the money they paid for it by selling seal furs to Europe. Then came the Klondyke gold rush, followed by oil discovery.

I decided to head for the lee of Little Diomede and by next morning was approaching the northern shore. I felt a thump under the boat. As I looked around I could see that I had hit a walrus. There were dozens of them swimming about. Weighing about one and a half tonnes with tusks a metre long, they are unusual creatures. Here they were lolling about in their familiar environment, quite unbothered by my strange boat and quite unconcerned about getting out of the way.

The island sheltered me from the gale-force wind and I was able to sit about 200 or 300 metres offshore under the shadow of rugged sheer cliffs. And here I witnessed a display I shall never forget.

Nesting in the cliffs, flying and circling overhead, were a million migratory sea birds. Thousands were in the air at any one time, and dozens of species screamed and fought each other and dived for fish as the nonchalant walruses watched the action, moving around, sticking their heads up out of the water.

It was an amphitheatre of birds. Swarms of black-legged kittiwakes poured through the air with their distinctive call – *kittee-wa-aaake, kitte-wa-aaake*. There were common and thick-billed murres with their black Batman-like hoods and capes over white feathers, and several species of auk including the crested auk. The least auklets, the smallest species, are only sparrow-sized but they plunge into the water in pursuit of their prey, thrusting and "flying" through the water. They must eat 86 per cent of their body weight each day, so you can imagine the frenzy from that species alone.

Every crevice in the rocks and cliffs had a bird on it. You'd see them come back in to land and they seemed to unerringly know where to go. Bigger birds had priority over the smaller ones, and of the ones circling there were always two or three that were aggressively attacking others with their talons. Dead birds floated about the boat.

It was like arriving at a concert – of birds, water, wind. A cacophony of sound, with just me and the walruses as the audience.

This was nature in its very essence – survival of the species, survival of the fittest. I have seen birds that swim and fish that fly. At times like this you can see and feel the power and miracle of nature. There's nothing gentle about it. It's just about survival. If a bird can't defend itself, it won't last, and so the strength of the species is continued.

What a place this was. And yet, for all its isolation, it is actually populated – the 2010 census showed 115 people lived here. The Inuit have had a settlement here for at least 3000 years.

When John Muir, the American naturalist and conservationist, visited the island in 1881 he wrote this:

"No margin is left for a village along the shore, so, like the seabirds that breed here and fly about in countless multitudes darkening the water, the rocks and the air, the Natives had to perch their huts on the cliffs, dragging boats and everything up and down steep trails. The huts are mostly of stone with skin roofs. They look like mere stone heaps, black dots on the snow at a distance, with whalebone posts set up and framed at the top to lay their canoes beyond the dogs that would otherwise eat them. The dreariest towns I ever beheld . . . the tops of the islands in gloomy storm clouds, snow to the water's edge, and blocks of rugged ice for a fringe; then the black water dashing against the ice; the gray sleety sky, the screaming water birds, the howling wind, and the blue gathering sludge."

Sailing alone definitely makes one philosophical. I think it's always been the way with sailors, so although I had different technology from that of earlier explorers such as Cook – or indeed John Muir – in many ways my experience was the same. I was watching nature in all its force, connected to tides and winds, sun and rain, close to birds and other sea creatures, and speculating about the nature of life.

Being out on the ocean, arriving at places like the Diomede Islands where life has continued in its patterns for probably millions of years, often made me think that the things we deem important aren't really so, especially in politics and management. The corridors of power: that side of life seemed small.

Out here life was very elemental. I was aware of the planet spinning, its relationship to the sun, the moon's orbit, the tides, the effect of wind on the ocean. The ebb and flow of the seasons. The Aurora Borealis. *Oh, there it is again* – you see it every night, just like you see the clouds in the sky.

These are the things we forget when we're busy with our normal lives in our busy cities.

I smiled as the latest weather forecast came in. "Wind diminishing by midnight". This fitted with my mood exactly. *Yes*, I thought, *we are diminishing.*

It was good news though, and once the wind eased I sailed away from the area. I could see walruses ahead but held my course, thinking they would move away. But no, thump again, almost stopping the boat. As I looked back, a huge creature with its head held high looked directly at me as if to say, "What are you doing in our territory?"

———

I had guessed a million birds. When I researched it later I found that indeed there are up to 1.3 million birds nesting there. I felt like the only person who had ever been in that place to see it, although of course I knew I wasn't. I wished I could share it – I really felt my aloneness at times like that. Sharing incredible experiences is so much a part of experiencing them yourself.

25

THE DEADLIEST SEA

In the midst of the gale I could do no more than look on, for what is a man in a storm like this?
—Joshua Slocum, *Sailing Alone Around the World*

Leaving the Diomede Islands, I sailed out of the Arctic Circle. It would take me about two days to reach St Lawrence Island, a large island thought to be the last remaining section of the ancient land bridge between Asia and North America, beyond which was the Bering Sea. I passed the Russian coast 25 miles to the west, with the small Alaskan city of Nome some 260 miles to the east.

It was now nearly five weeks since I'd left Nuuk. The chilly bin was empty, but my remaining stock of food included: 33 soups, 26 tinned meals, plenty of rice, mashed potato, onions, carrots, eggs, salami, tinned tuna, bread, milk, coffee and tea. Supplies were looking good, especially if I caught a few fish to have as either sashimi, fried or curried.

Nights were getting longer. The Aurora Borealis was still entertaining me on the odd clear night. As I passed the International Dateline, clocks moved a day ahead and as I turned the clock back an hour at 6pm, great news: another happy hour at 5pm!

The wind was 15–20 knots SSE and I made slow progress towards St Lawrence Island. The sea temperature was 1.6 degrees, with a toasty 3.5 inside my cabin, but I was pleased to be sailing in deeper water now – around 65–75 metres. Finally, St Lawrence Island's grey cliffs passed by a few miles to port.

It was time to run the gauntlet across the Bering Sea to the Aleutian Islands, 400 miles to the south.

The Bering Sea is one of the most dangerous bodies of water in the world. It has a strong current flowing north and is subject to regular storm and gale warnings, with the strongest storms occurring during August and September. Fishing in this area, while an industry of major importance, is quoted as the deadliest job in the United States. The Discovery Channel's popular television show *The Deadliest Catch* captures life here. Many lives are lost and many yachts and ships have rolled and come to grief in this area. The National Weather Service frequently reports hazardous weather conditions with some storms described as "epic magnitude". Forecasters often warn of 9–12-metre waves. There is no question it is one of the stormiest places on earth.

I had been aware for a couple of days of weather bombs approaching from the west, from off the coast of Japan and Siberia – low-pressure systems that just keep coming, one after another. Now typhoons were forming. They were proceeding northwest to become gale-force cyclones in the area between my present position and where I was heading, the Aleutian Islands chain now about 350 miles south.

The Aleutians are a chain of islands that scatter in an arc across 1200 miles off the Alaskan Peninsula, spreading like a necklace towards

Russia. They form the boundary between the Bering Sea and the North Pacific Ocean. They were part of the arena of war against the Japanese in the Second World War. Adak Island in the western Aleutians was an American military base from 1942 until the 1990s, the area contaminated by chemical ammunitions dumping. It's disused now and a clean-up is underway, but I couldn't help wondering how it affected the fish. PCBs and DDT-related compounds have been found in green-winged teal, bald eagles, sea otters and mussels from Adak, according to the US Fish and Wildlife Service, although the source for these compounds is not clear. That's another realisation from my journey – that no matter how isolated a place is, it will not be unaffected by climate change or by other effects of our industrialised world.

My ideal course was south towards these islands, and I was hoping to sail through one of several island passes midway in the Aleutian chain, then into the Pacific Ocean and on a course for home.

However, with rough seas and winds now 30–40 knots and blowing from the southwest, I was only able to make a course east of south. I was going to be meeting the Aleutians further east than I'd hoped.

But I didn't have time to worry about that. I was in a gale. I had two reefs in the mainsail and the smallest headsail up, and it was like sailing over hills. I had secured everything below in case of a roll-over, but so far, with the waves quite wide apart, *Astral Express* was handling the conditions okay – in fact slightly better than I was.

There was no let-up, and as the hours and then days went by with the wind hammering and capsize always imminent, I was becoming frustrated. It was pointless to feel that way – as if human feelings could affect the gale – but it was becoming hard not to feel frustrated, with so much constant effort being demanded and so little progress. It was like hitting my head against a wall. I had by now taken the mainsail down, and had only the headsail up. It was relentless.

The wind increased up to 65–70 knots. I took all sails down and got the sea anchor ready. My computer bounced across the cabin after being dislodged from its Velcro strips with the crashing motion. Not much fun, but I somehow managed to get my sense of humour back. I was glad I'd had the chance to test the boat out during Hurricane Harvey. Knowing she handled that storm made me confident we would survive the Bering Sea.

I went outside to check the rigging, check the sea, make sure everything was tied down properly. If the wind eased at all I put some sail up, rolled a bit of headsail out. I was monitoring all the time for those opportunities. I observed how the waves were hitting the boat, whether they were slipping underneath or whether I needed to alter the course at all in response to changing conditions.

With autopilot you don't make a human response to every wave. You get your boat on a course that feels comfortable – in this case with the wind on the quarter, so that the waves came sort of on the side but slightly behind so that the boat would come up and the waves would slip underneath. Once you've been doing it for three or four hours and you know the wind strength is staying the same and the boat's handling it, you set the autopilot so the boat can continue on a course that feels comfortable with the sea.

I was making slow progress in a semi-favourable direction, which was better than going too fast in the wrong direction. You have to do whatever's safe, and if something is necessary, that's what you do.

With mountainous seas and curling, breaking waves I escaped back into the cabin and turned the music up to drown out the screaming noise outside. Happy music – songs with a bounce to match the movement of the boat. Elvis Presley was a favourite for these conditions, and I turned him up loud and we rode the waves together.

All I could do was hang on. The handrails inside were invaluable. I'd installed them everywhere because if you don't hold on as you move about in this kind of gale, you will either be dead or at least severely injured. The boat lurched and jerked violently and constantly. It was impossible to predict which way it was going to move next. If I hadn't hung on I'd have been flung against something and broken a limb or got concussed. I've had enough of this, I thought. This is dangerous. Please let it ease.

But the seas continued to gather up to second-spreader height, which is about nine metres. Luckily the waves were well apart as it had been blowing for days, but about every seventh one broke, sometimes in front, sometimes at the rear, sometimes side on, drenching the deck but fortunately sliding underneath the boat.

I was so grateful for the leather helm seat, a great comfort and support in conditions like these. I could strap myself into it for a rest, or take a few minutes shut-eye by leaning on the back of it, hanging on.

It was impossible to cook in this weather, so I was once again living on coffee, soup, cheese, chocolate and biscuits.

At night it was pitch black outside, but the screaming of the wind in the rigging continued, as did the smashing and roaring of the sea. The wind was increasing. The boat shuddered and bucked as it took an especially big hit. I had covered 145 miles under bare poles in 24 hours.

I knew I had the boat set up right, and at night all I could do was trust I wasn't going to get a rogue wave that would roll me over. There wasn't a lot I could do about that. I'd set it up as best I could, and it felt fine. I could see from the wind gauge, the speed of the boat and the direction that I was going okay. If anything changed, I would feel it as well as see it. I was very attuned to the boat, to the howling weather outside.

Astral Express was handling it.

Storm, storm, storm. I was a week battling that storm. Every now and then it would ease up, then the blast would come again. *You can run but you can't hide.* And I'd be back to bare poles. My daily runs were in the low 100s, but at least it was progress.

After several days I determined a course for Sanak Strait, on the eastern end of the Aleutians between Sanak Island and the rest of the Fox group. I was feeling battered. My nerves were somewhat frayed, but I knew that with a bit of a rest I'd be in great shape. There was some small respite between these never-ending low-pressure systems sliding across from the west, one after the other, and the sea was feeling a little easier. I set some sail and inched my way forward. The barometer had stopped falling and the wind was WSW 30–40 knots. The stay sail was torn, the dodger (cockpit cover) had blown out – but what a great boat *Astral Express* was proving to be. The waves had stopped breaking but the huge swells in this area never stopped.

Sanak Strait was about 120 miles east of where my ideal course would have been. I wasn't too worried about that. In fact, being a little further east in the Pacific would put me in a good position for the trade winds that tended to blow from the east (NE in the Northern Hemisphere and SE below the equator).

However, the respite was short lived and as I approached Sanak Strait the wind got up to 50 knots again. It was a relief to get into the strait, with the wind easing in the shelter of the islands, still whistling over the top but the water fairly calm. It was about 20 miles through between the islands, the strait about five miles wide, and I slowed things up and got about seven hours to tidy up and rest.

I was now so close to the Pacific, an encouraging thought. Home waters! I couldn't wait, even though I still had 5000 miles to go.

I passed several crab fishing boats also sheltering among the islands, and over the radio I heard there had been a helicopter rescue in the area. Hell hath no fury like a low in the Aleutians.

Towards the southern end of Sanak Strait I passed an anchored fishing boat sheltering from the storm. I spoke to the skipper by radio and he informed me of a town nearby with a supermarket. "I'm sailing non-stop to Auckland," I told him. "I've just sailed through the Northwest Passage."

"You must be crazy," he said.

"Not as crazy as you, fishing in these waters," I thought to myself. Within a month reports in this area would be of ice.

Throughout the trip I spoke to Edward every day. He called me just as I was coming through the Aleutians. "It's a good day," I told him.

"Why's that?"

"The boat's insured again."

I could never get over the incredible generosity of Edward in letting me sail his boat, that he trusted me not to sink it or write it off. I don't really believe in luck – usually, the secret is in the planning – but meeting Edward and him first buying the boat and then letting me have it back: that was pure luck.

By evening the wind had eased a little so I decided to push on into the Pacific. To begin with I had about 35 knots of wind and just the smallest possible sails set, but in no time it had increased again. Another weather bomb exploded over me and soon it was blowing 50 knots and gusting up to sixty. It was too much wind for my sail so down it came again, and I set a course ESE with the gale coming in from the west.

I'm a calm person. "Cool, calm and collected", my daughter Rebecca says of me. She reckons nothing ever fazes me, and it's true. Like most ocean-going sailors, I just deal with matters as they arise and I'm logical rather than emotional. Like a lot of sailors I guess I underplay things – I'll talk about a breeze when it's a 40-knot wind.

My logbook for this trip is mostly pretty businesslike – a record of longitude and latitude, wind speed and short observations on sea and landscape. But on that day I sailed into the Pacific and the seemingly relentless gale escalated, I allowed myself a bit of emotion.

"Horrific seas," I wrote, with uncharacteristic fervour, my pen pushing dark against the paper, my writing scrawling slightly against the movement of the boat. And: "Had headsail problem last night. Wrapped MPS halyard. Fixed when daylight – scary." And three days later: "Bad night."

The boat was handling okay but the seas were enormous, the biggest I had ever seen. Waves surged to about 9–12 metres, with the odd one breaking and noisy. The wind veered more to the north as I veered south, so I ran off a little more after taking a big hit with a wave crashing over the whole boat. Funny – as I looked out the back of the boat the seas didn't look so bad. But now the wind increased again, up to 55 and 65 knots. This was not a good place. *What's going on?* Surely it would ease in maybe another hour. It was howling.

At least the autopilot was doing a good job. As night fell it was pitch black again. I just had to trust the boat and run with it – running blind through nine-metre waves.

By morning the wind had eased a little. I had the mainsail aluminium boom tied with a rope to prevent it crashing across in an accidental jibe. To release it I would have to cut it and retie it. I could see this knotted rope, this frayed effigy, through the window as it bounced and danced with the motion of the sea in a style similar to my friend Lydia. With the music up loud to drown out the noise of the storm, I tried dancing and singing inside to take my mind off things while Lydia danced outside.

Finally, the storm subsided, or perhaps I finally sailed away from it. It was moving NE and I was heading SE. I was now at 175°43' west and 39°57' north. As the day went by the seas went down, and with light winds from the northerly quarter over the next few days the complexion on board changed for the better. During the last part of the storm I covered 140 miles with no sail up at all.

What a big day at the office this had been. Get me out of this place!

I set my course for New Zealand.

26

THE CALM AFTER THE STORM

He moana pukepuke e ekengia e te waka
A stormy sea can be navigated
—Maori proverb

It's lucky in life that we forget the crappy experiences and soon start to feel good again. I had persevered through some of the biggest seas in the world, and now, as the winds dropped at last and the seas went down, it was hard to believe I was on the same planet.

The sky cleared and that evening I saw a green flash at sunset. What a treat – this is a rare phenomenon that happens when the sun is almost entirely below a cloudless horizon, with just its barest edge still visible and, for just a second or two, that upper rim appears green. The briefest flash. Many people never see it.

Battered and bruised, it was a relief for me to take things quietly and to restore a sense of order aboard *Astral Express*. I dried things out and got some jobs done on deck. I repaired the staysail and noted that the sails were generally in great shape. A new mainsail had been put on in the Faroe Islands, and Edward had had the headsail replaced.

The other main storm damage was to the cockpit dodger, and I retied and retaped that. I put the anchor away, taped the windlass and mast. I put a new bolt in the boom vang, the rod that holds the main boom in place, and fixed a leak in the fuel breather. I put up and untangled the MPS, pumped the bilges, did an engine check and, happily, took the covers off the stainless-steel handles now that the air had become a little warmer.

I checked the autopilot motor. I had used four of these over my so-far 22,000 miles, mainly because in accidental jibes the motor overworked against the rudder stops and stripped the plastic cogs.

At last there was no condensation left on the inside windows. Everything was dry. There wasn't a cloud in the sky and the stars were a gentle carpet. Sea temperature was up to 22 degrees, I had my fishing line out and my shorts on. Everything was back to normal, even me.

I saw another green flash at sunset. This was magic.

I could hardly believe the change. Behind me those horrible low-pressure weather bombs were still pounding the Bering Sea, but ahead of me I had good weather forecast.

There was lots of bird life. Little ones fluttered like butterflies while the albatross hardly moved its wings as it glided gracefully to catch fish – it really was the 747 of birds. The food it caught gave it the energy to keep catching fish. Were we on the same treadmill, too?

By 1 October and the sixth week out from Nuuk, the NE trade winds had set in as I approached the western Hawaiian islands.

Midway Island is the most western of the Hawaiian chain, and I sighted it 12 miles away to my starboard side as the trade winds carried me briskly along and I started to make regular daily runs of about 175 nautical miles. As the wind freshened I put all possible weight to port, and pumped the fuel across to that side.

Sea temperature was now 29 degrees.

I had plenty of fuel and water, although food choices were fewer now, but I knew I had enough for the run home. Mahimahi was on the menu at present. The bad memories from the Bering Sea were easily replaced with these good times.

During the Northwest Passage I was on edge and high alert all the time and all I was thinking about was getting out of there, knowing that by the end of September it would all change for the worse when it iced up again. I felt I was in foreign, almost sacred, territory – in a way that I was in forbidden waters. Now I was heading for home.

As I looked at the wake behind the boat I started to feel happy. Each mile that went past was a mile closer to New Zealand. The equator was ahead. Cotton wool clouds puffed overhead, a 20-knot trade wind helped me on my way, and I basked outside at 33° degrees.

It's a long equator from 74° north.

27

THE BEAUTIFUL
SOUTH PACIFIC

Coal-black seas towered up on all sides, and a glittering myriad of tropical stars drew a faint reflection from plankton in the water. The world was simple – stars in the darkness. Whether it was 1947 BC or AD suddenly became of no significance. We lived, and that we felt with alert intensity . . . We were swallowed up in the absolute common measure of history – endless unbroken darkness under a swarm of stars.

—Thor Heyerdahl, *Kon Tiki: Across the Pacific by Raft*

Awareness of global warming, or climate change as it's now being called, is featuring everywhere. My view and observation is that all pollution is bad for the planet, and I did notice more of it in the Northern

Hemisphere. More rubbish in the water, more air travel, more ships, a hazier atmosphere – it's all worse in the Northern Hemisphere, which is not surprising as 90 per cent of the world's population lives there. It is a marked contrast to the Southern Hemisphere with its cleaner water and clearer skies. It is almost as if we have two worlds, the north and the south.

The winds were variable and with an easterly current going against the wind the sailing had become uncomfortable as I headed ever-further south. But I had an easy time of it in the doldrums and got through okay, crossing the equator after 12 days on port tack. It was a great feeling to be in the Southern Hemisphere.

I remembered what Joshua Slocum wrote about being on the equator: "Many think it is excessively hot right under the sun. It is not necessarily so. As a matter of fact the thermometer stands at a bearable point whenever there is a breeze and a ripple on the sea, even exactly under the sun. It is often hotter in cities and on sandy shores in higher latitudes." For me, crowded cities seemed far away.

The water was now clear and I had left the rubbish behind – the last I saw was in the current eddies north of the equator. I kept all my own non-biodegradable rubbish bagged up on board. There wasn't a lot of it, but at the end of the first leg I did take a bagful ashore when I first arrived at Nuuk, and I had another small bag of it when I arrived in Auckland.

Even this close to the equator, the Southern Hemisphere seemed clearer – less pollution in the water, clear skies. The starry, starry nights were a treat. Where did they come from, I wondered, as generations of sailors have wondered before me. This was sailors' business – dwelling on the nature of infinity, and musing on our great and diverse world.

I spoke to Peter Semotiuk of Cambridge Bay in the central Northwest Passage who informed me that by 3 October it had frozen and was dark almost all day. I looked around at the blue Pacific, at the light glinting off the swell. The sun was high in the sky, blessing me with 30 degrees.

I had scarcely any clothes on. I felt a rush of pure happiness not to be stuck in ice up there. Oh, the relief of the South Pacific.

I was now 2700 miles away from home, around 15 days by my estimation. My course would take me to the west of Fiji. Tahiti would be well out to port, which was just as well as if it was any closer I might have been tempted to stop there. My nirvana. I've always had a special feeling for Tahiti.

Mathieu Bonnier called from France on 12 October, enquiring about my progress and apologising for not being able to come to New Zealand to see me arrive. Edward rang to say he and his family would be there when I sailed into Auckland.

The pressure was on and tension was mounting. I was very aware that a small breakage or mishap could still jeopardise a good run home. I thought about how different it was for the America's Cup sailors who concentrate on only one job each. Their boats are taken out of the water every night and serviced, while the sailors go home to their partners to be pampered after a hard day – and they get paid for it.

Strange that even after so long at sea and having become so used to sailing alone, I still sometimes woke up to an alarm and – just for a split second – thought that someone else would sort it out. Then: "No, it's only me."

The night-time alarms were often the radar letting me know that a rain squall was coming through. These were frequent, blowing in every four hours or so. They showed up on radar about eight miles away and the alarm would go off, so I had time to get on deck, put a reef in the main, and roll up the headsail a little before the wind and rain came in. The wind usually increased from 20 knots to about 30, accompanied by a downpour and some thunder and lightning – and then it would be gone. During the day they were easy to deal with. It is more pleasant out in the rain, and easy to run off during the squalls. Collecting rainwater was a bonus which meant at least one more shower.

News of my progress was filtering into the New Zealand media, and I was starting to get journalists from radio, newspapers and magazines calling. Communication with Variety indicated quite a few donations from all over the world – that was pleasing, as although the Variety fundraising had been such a feature of the first leg of the trip, it had lost impetus during the break and now, of course, the boat no longer carried the Variety logo. But it was good to know there was still interest and that I was raising some money.

Meanwhile, I managed to avoid the hundreds of islands that dot this part of the Pacific, and with the trade winds helping, Fiji's Yasawa Islands could soon be seen out to port. I now had 1100 miles to go to Auckland.

Just keep it cool, I said to myself, and bring her home.

I was so close to completing this trip. The worst thing that could happen now was some small technical thing would make me have to pull in somewhere to get it fixed. The boat had done a lot of work now, so what had worn? What could break? I had always been very careful to check everything, leaving nothing to chance.

It would only take something like a broken rudder to spell the end, but all the original aspects of the boat's design seemed to be fine. In fact, it wasn't until a few years later, with *Astral Express* now owned by someone else altogether, that the rudder finally needed rebuilding. The new owner was just setting out from Auckland to cruise in the Pacific. He was on his knees vomiting over the back, and when he finished he was sitting there and looking at the rudder and could see some unwarranted motion, some cracking in the fibreglass. Luckily, he hadn't gone far, and he turned around and came back. Philip Wilson then spent five or six days rebuilding the rudder gudgeon, fitted it back, and off they went. I think about how that original rudder went all those

185

thousands of miles, so it actually did pretty well.

But it was just as well I was so careful about checking everything because, sure enough, I found something that could have been a problem.

Doing a general check of the boat, I lifted up the engine hatches and checked the bilges, and then thought I'd check the engine's oil. But when I pulled the dipstick up, water came out of it.

Being on port tack for so many days with the exhaust outlet on the downwind side close to the water, back pressure had caused seawater to syphon in. I had caught it just in time. I quickly took off hoses near the engine and was able to drain the water out, and then I changed the oil, changed the filters and there was no problem. It was lucky because if I had tried to start the engine with water in it I could have broken it. To deal with it I found that a plastic drinking cup fitted the exhaust pipe perfectly and with a tap in with the hammer, problem solved. I just had to remember to take it off when using the engine.

I needed the engine not for moving along – I did the entire journey under sail as planned – but for charging my batteries to run my communication systems, radar and so on. I didn't know until I got back that the alternator on the engine was not charging. I got home because the wind generator and solar panels were working and they gave me so much power that I wasn't even aware that the big alternator was not kicking in. I had plenty of fuel left and was only running the engine about once a week anyway.

The main casualty of the engine drama was that in the rush to turn off intakes and remove hoses, I lacerated my arm, cutting it on the sharp edges of plastic cable ties. They were small cuts but my arm was completely red. I soon had it mummified with a bandage. It looked a lot worse than it really was, and it healed within a day or so.

Having a good medical kit on board was so important, and it really didn't need to be complicated. In fact, in an emergency when sailing on your own, it's best that it's not. For that reason I had earlier taken out all the strong painkillers to have them within easy reach should a problem occur, as taking those first could make a self-diagnosis and repair a little easier.

The only other job I needed to do at that late stage was to climb part way up the mast and replace sail slides. An easy job in the marina, out there in the ocean the constant motion made it half a day's work.

―――――

With Fiji now astern, I was on the home run. I began to allow myself to think that getting to Auckland was a distinct possibility. I could almost see the Sky Tower – only 800 miles to go.

With hopefully just six days to go I did another check: navigation gear okay, both autopilots okay, engine and batteries okay, sails and rig okay.

In the morning I found flying fish on deck. They can fly for about 100 metres but crash into the boat when it is dark. They're edible but I never did try them. They're very small, like a herring, and you'd need two or three to make a meal.

On the whole circumnavigation I had caught and eaten only 18 fish.

I tidied my food locker. What did I have left? Plenty of rice, pasta and soup. Two-minute noodles, milk, coffee. Biscuits. Six tins of meat dinner and tins of carrots and beans. Water – six drinking bottles and some in the tank. Three beers and a quarter of a bottle of rum. The choices had become fairly minimal but it wouldn't be true to say there was anything I was particularly missing. I was aware that it would be nice to have a choice of food, or to have someone else cook it for me, but I knew that would happen soon enough. I thought about going to a restaurant and having a choice of 10 different dishes. Too much choice, I decided.

The only thing I perhaps missed was a long, hot shower – to linger under the hot water without having to hang on for dear life. Now, that's a luxury.

I washed a few clothes and put some fresh ones aside for my arrival. I bagged up my arctic gear, and the interior started to look a little bare, if not clean and tidy.

With 400 miles to go I was really getting nervous. So close, but now with lumpy seas and varying light headwinds I was only making about 110 miles per day. A breakage now could be disastrous. I checked every-thing again.

On Saturday 23 October an easterly wind came in and I could hold course for the Northland east coast of New Zealand. Nice sailing, and now with an estimated time of arrival of 27 October.

I was having trouble sleeping – I might have been getting excited about completing this monumental journey. You have to finish what you start. I had covered 9700 miles since leaving Nuuk. Messages were coming in, saying things like: "ranks amongst the greatest seafaring voyages", "historical navigation", "maritime record-breaking epoch". But wait – I wasn't home yet.

Mathieu called again to give me encouragement. I was conscious that I was enjoying my sailing, enjoying the last few days.

Only 200 miles to go. I ate soup again and was now wearing clothes as the days had become cooler. Roll on Auckland. It had been a struggle getting through the last few degrees. *I'm glad the world isn't any larger.*

Home seemed a long way back there with 700 miles to go and headwinds, but now I could almost smell the sheep.

On the morning of 26 October I sighted land – the beautiful Poor Knights Islands about 30 miles ahead, themselves just 14 miles offshore of New Zealand's northern east coast. What a great way to complete what had been a most amazing journey for mind and soul, not to mention body and boat: to arrive in New Zealand waters on a beautiful morning, with calm sea, light wind, clear sky. The familiar birds of home were like old friends – the white-fronted terns, flocks of small grey-and-white

Cook's petrel, and their larger black cousins. With an escort of dolphins, the barometer high and a good weather forecast, it was as if Nature was giving me a pat on the back.

28

HOME

He who returns from a journey is not the same as he who left.
—Chinese proverb

After encountering every extreme during this 10,000-mile part of the circumnavigation, with 24 hours to go and at last fairly confident I was going to make it, I slowed things up a little. I wanted to savour the moment. I had a shower, gave myself a haircut, got out some clean clothes. I might have had a rum except that I had run out a few days before. I didn't miss it. Every empty bottle was sent overboard with a position and a message inside.

I was on a private high of pride.

As I sailed south I crossed the path I took back in 2005 and I recorded a total of 28,000 miles for the complete journey. I felt what anyone must feel who has achieved an ultimate goal – it's an incredible feeling, very special, private and surprisingly humbling. I certainly allowed myself a great sense of achievement.

On a nice Wednesday morning, 27 October 2010, I sailed casually into the Hauraki Gulf and on into the Waitemata Harbour. The sea was calm and there was a light easterly. I knew I had a big day ahead.

The phone had been hot with radio interviews and word of my arrival had got out. Vessels were tooting as they passed by.

During the friendly Customs clearance a local TV crew come aboard for an interview and they arranged a live broadcast for later that evening. They gave me a bag of apples and a cold beer, very welcome gifts.

That done, I was free to motor around to the Viaduct Basin in the CBD of Auckland where I had been allocated a visitor's berth for a few days. There waiting on the dock for me was a happy crowd of family and friends, along with the Commodore and representatives of the Royal New Zealand Yacht Squadron, and the Mayor of Auckland. I was particularly pleased to see my partner and Edward, Birgit and their son Simun. Without their incredible understanding and generosity I could not have completed my adventure.

Des Dillon from Soul Bar and Restaurant, a popular Viaduct eaterie, came down the gangway holding a tray of champagne – a fine gesture and a great way to celebrate my homecoming.

Everyone possible came on board to inspect the boat, especially Edward.

By evening the television crew had done their second interview and a group of us enjoyed dinner together at Soul Bar. I must admit that I was still a bit wobbly on my feet. I enjoyed the food that I didn't have to cook myself, but I didn't eat too much. That would change, I knew. I had missed the socialising and I knew that I would linger in the hot shower where I didn't have to hold on.

The next morning after getting over the festivities I came down to *Astral Express* about 11am. I hosed down the decks, filled the water tank, and took Edward, family and friends for an afternoon sail on Auckland Harbour. I was so pleased that the boat was in such good shape I could take it for a cruise like this the day after arriving from a 10,000-mile adventure. Edward had already been here a week before I arrived and was soon to fly out. It was so special to have him and his family come down to New Zealand and it made my arrival even more special. Thanks again, Edward.

Thanks to all those involved, from the Ancient Mariner.

There was a lot of media coverage of my journey both nationally and internationally, especially relating to my sailing of the Northwest Passage. They said things like: "The Everest of sailing"; "Fastest sailing of NWP"; "One of the most dangerous routes in the world"; "The Northwest Passage considered a watery Everest"; "Most extensive solo circumnavigation ever undertaken". Many emails followed that used words like respect, brave, envious, balls, guts, ultimate classroom, satisfaction, trepidation, inspirational, courage, inspiring, journey of a lifetime, inspiration to over-60s, a tribute to your planning, fantastic cause, and so on.

This was all very nice but the private feeling I carried towards my achievement was harder to explain. Following my first effort in 2005 I had felt untouchable – ten feet tall and bulletproof. Now I felt quieter and more humble. I would have expected it to be the other way around. Maybe it was because I'd been shaped by my experiences in the Northwest Passage. I felt more vulnerable there. In a place like that, you know you're mortal. It had a big impact on me. Being trapped in ice, running aground, being in such a remote area, then enduring that final storm afterwards . . .

But I never had self-doubt. I never doubted that I should keep going, or that I would make it out. I knew when I was in a predicament that if I didn't do the right thing I would be in trouble, but I always had a Plan B or a Plan C. I always knew that whatever was necessary would follow if I used my head and kept calm.

I understood now how others felt when they achieved their ultimate goal. For instance, if someone won an Olympic gold medal, they were obviously celebrated in public, but now I understood that it would be the feeling inside that person – their personal satisfaction – that would be the real mark of achievement. No matter what the media or anyone else says, you have that feeling inside yourself and nobody can ever take that away. It's personal knowledge – you've set yourself a goal, and you've been able to achieve it.

The important thing here is that we can have dreams but we must also have a goal, or a target. If you don't create a target, you've got nothing to hit. I had a vision and then I set myself a target, and I worked towards it with preparation and determination. So that's what I say to others who also have dreams: hang on to your vision, but turn it into a goal that you can plot your way towards.

I am often asked what I will do next.

I chose to test myself on the longest, hardest sailing course that I could think of. No-one else has ever done it. I'm happy with that; it has ticked the box.

There must be people who work all their lives to do something and when they've done it have a hollow feeling, a vacuum where their ambition used to be. I don't, probably because of my age. I'm at an age where I don't need to yearn to do anything else – but you never know!

There are risks in attempting our dreams – emotional risks, physical risks. But I'd say it's important to try. You can't be put off by risk alone.

We need to encourage exploration and the testing of limits. Sure, there were physical risks in my journey. I could have got iced in up in the Northwest Passage; I could have lost my boat in a storm.

The fact that those things didn't happen I put down mostly to meticulous research and preparation. That's what you do with risk – you find out about it and work your way around it. You don't let it stop you at the first hurdle. I always said, from the very outset, that if something came along that was unworkable I would drop my plan. But that didn't happen.

Chop your own wood, and it will warm you twice, the great industrialist Henry Ford said. I couldn't agree more. This was a solo journey from its inception all those years ago in the holiday home in the Marlborough Sounds to the day I sailed back into the Waitemata Harbour with all the planet's oceans behind me. I enjoyed the expert input of others and the personal support of my family. But all the decision-making and planning was my own, and when it came to carrying out my plans I was on my own. It was the ultimate in self-reliance, and therefore double the reward in terms of my feeling of achievement.

I sailed around the world, and I did it by myself.

———

The Northwest Passage was the best sailing experience of my life. It was such a great feeling to achieve what many have tried to do, and my thoughts are with those who perished while trying to find that route in the early days.

The birds and animals that live there, the crazy ice formations and massive barren landscapes coupled with the sense of impending winter all made it an awesome place of beauty, scary at times, yet indelibly exciting – the ultimate test of seamanship.

From Lancaster Sound to Barrow Point was 1782 miles. I was the first person ever to sail the Northwest Passage solo non-stop, and I did it at an average speed of 146 miles per day over 12 days, the fastest-ever-recorded time.

To incorporate this fabled passage during a solo circumnavigation of the globe was a big bonus.

Sailing from Auckland to Nuuk in 2005 took 124 days and covered 18,300 miles. In 2010 I completed the 10,000-mile voyage from Nuuk to Auckland in 68 days with an average of 148 miles per day, which was similar to my speed on the outward journey. My average speed over the entire journey was six and a quarter knots.

Altogether, over both legs I sailed a total of 192 days and covered 32 oceans and seaways.

Stage 1:
Pacific Ocean
Tasman Sea
Coral Sea
Pollard Channel
Great Barrier Reef
Torres Strait
Gulf of Carpentaria
Arafura Sea
Timor Sea
Indian Ocean
Southern Ocean
South Atlantic
North Atlantic
Labrador Sea
Davis Strait
Baffin Sea

Stage 2:

Davis Strait

Baffin Sea

Lancaster Sound

Barrow Strait

Peel Sound

Franklin Strait

Victoria Strait

Queen Maude Gulf

Dease Strait

Coronation Gulf

Dolphin and Union Strait

Amundsen Gulf

Beaufort Sea

Arctic Ocean

Chukchi Sea

Bering Strait

Bering Sea

Pacific Ocean

I was very proud to receive some prestigious awards and recognition for my sailing achievements. I received the Yachting New Zealand Cruising Award from the Royal New Zealand Yacht Squadron in 2010 and I was mentioned in *National Geographic* as one of the top global adventurers of 2010.

Then in the 2012 New Year Honours I was awarded the New Zealand Order of Merit (MNZM) "for outstanding services to sailing and philanthropy". The award was presented by the Governor-General Sir Jerry Mateparae, and the presentation read:

"In 2010 Mr Graeme Kendall completed a solo circumnavigation from Auckland to Auckland, via the Northwest Passage. The course covered 28,000 miles and 32 oceans and seaways. He was the first person to sail the Northwest Passage solo non-stop. Known by sailors as the Everest of the sailing world, the Arctic Northwest Passage is only open for a short time every year because of pack ice, and is known for treacherous waters. Mr Kendall sailed through the Passage in just 12 days, one of the shortest times for the Passage ever. His journey rates as one of New Zealand's great expedition achievements. During his trip he raised funds for Children's Charity. Mr Kendall received the Yachting New Zealand Cruising Award from the Royal New Zealand Yacht Squadron and the *National Geographic* Award for being one of the top global adventurers in 2010. Graeme Kendall, MNZM – for services to sailing and philanthropy."

Going to the ceremony was a great experience for my partner and children. I wished that my parents could have been there.

EPILOGUE

With *Astral Express* now all the way down at the other end of the Earth, Edward decided to sell her. Early in 2011 *Astral Express* had her equipment serviced and was prepared for sale. Philip Wilson, my original Auckland project manager, continues to take care of the boat for the new owners. Only small changes have ever been made. She now has a refrigerator and a small dining table inside; the pipe berths have been removed and there's a settee with nice upholstery. But these changes are cosmetic; the structure of the boat has not been altered, and this is a tribute to the original design.

And still the good old leather helm seat remains.

In all of my sailing experience, birds never featured as prominently as during this voyage. They kept me company over all the oceans, sharing the forces of wind and current. I felt a real affinity with them, and watching them gave me hours of pleasure. What a thrill to discover this poem from the American poet Emily Dickinson.

"Hope" is the thing with feathers

"Hope" is the thing with feathers -
That perches in the soul -
And sings the tune without the words -
And never stops - at all -

And sweetest - in the Gale - is heard -
And sore must be the storm -
That could abash the little Bird
That kept so many warm -

I've heard it in the chillest land -
And on the strangest Sea -
Yet - never - in Extremity,
It asked a crumb - of me.
—*Emily Dickinson*

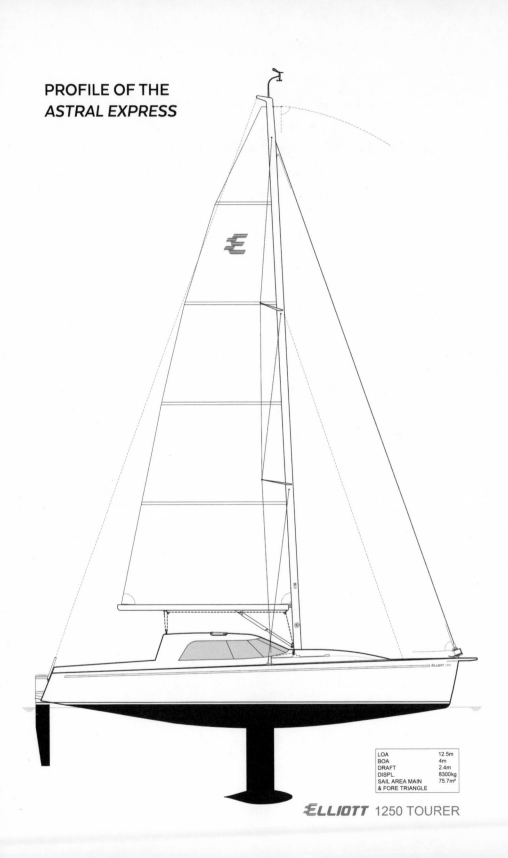

PROFILE OF THE
ASTRAL EXPRESS

LOA	12.5m
BOA	4m
DRAFT	2.4m
DISPL.	8300kg
SAIL AREA MAIN & FORE TRIANGLE	75.7m²

ELLIOTT 1250 TOURER

ACKNOWLEDGEMENTS

My thanks goes to Roger Badham, Ross Blackman, Inge Bo Johansen, Jesper Bo Johansen, Mathieu Bonnier, Murray Dean, Des Dillon, Greg Elliott, Bill Gee, Jessie Kendall, Joel Kendall, Nathan Kendall, Rebecca Kendall, Ruth Kendall, Peter Mytton, Terry Needham, Peter Newman, Birgit Niclasen, Dánjal Niclasen, Edward Niclasen, Jørgen Niclasen, Hevør Niclasen, Niclas Niclasen, Simun Niclasen, Jeni Pearce, Stan Pearson, Gareth Ramage, Royal New Zealand Yacht Squadron, Dave Schnackenburg, Tom Schnackenburg, Peter Semotiuk, Peter Stewart, Judith Tabron, Peter Talley, Philip Wilson and Lydia Zaicek. Further thanks to Franceska Marsic, Margie Thomson, Stephanie Van Oijen and Geoff Walker.

Inspiration from Captain Cook, Sir Peter Blake, Tiger Woods and Bob Dylan.

LIST OF PROVISIONS

The following list of provisions for Graeme Kendall on *Astral Express* was prepared for Graeme by dietician Jeni Pierce. This list covers the first four weeks of the voyage.

	Breakfast	Snack	Lunch	Dinner	Extras
WEEK 1	Sultana bran	Soup	Mac cheese	Beef curry 90g	Jerky 15g
	FD apple 25g	Le snak	Satay beef 300g	Lamb fettucine 90g	Cordial
	FD porridge 120g	Choc 50g	Chicken 300g	Roast chicken 175g	Jerky 25g
	FD muesli 150g	Gingernut 250g	Udon noodle 200g	Apricot chicken 90g	Tea 31 bags
	xx	Gum 14g	Baked beans 420g	Tika chicken 90g	Cheese spread
		Instant noodle	Tuna 85g	Fresh meal	Juice conc
		Muesli bar	Salmon 100g	Fresh meal	Loaf bread
		Fruit cake	Fresh meal	Hash potato 30g	Skim milk 400g
		Fruit x 3	Fresh meal	Mash potato 30g	
				Veges mixed 25g	

	Breakfast	Snack	Lunch	Dinner	Extras
WEEK 2	Scrambled egg 40g	Gingernut 250g	Mac cheese	Chicken pasta 300g	Full milk pwd 400g
	Porridge 800g	Digestive 250g	Satay beef pp 300g	Baboyjie 90g	Milo 350g
	Cooked bkft 90g	Cashew 40g	Pp chick	Roast lamb 90g	Loaf bread
	FD apple 25g	100g raisin nut	Uncle Ben rice 250g	Mexican chicken	Prune 340g
		Soup	Tuna 85g	Country beef 90g	Milkshake 220g
	Porridge	Le snak	Salmon 100g	Tika chicken 90g	Cordial
		Kit kat 17g	Dol pasta 215g	Teriyaki beef 90g	Juice conc
		Muesli bar	Dol mush sc 90g	Hash potato 30g	Jerky 15g
		Gum 14g	Can Irish stew 400g	Mash potato 30g	Jerky 25g
		Candy lollies		Vege 1	Jerky 30g
		Noodles 85g		Vege 2	Jerky 50g
WEEK 3	Apricot FD 25g	Soup	Mac cheese	Lamb 90g	Tea 31 bags
	Strawberry FD 25g	Licorice 190g	Satay beef 300g	Apricot chicken 90g	Jerky 15g
	Cornflakes 300g	Le snack	Chicken 300g	Thai chicken 90g	Jerky 25g
	FD muesli 150g	Raisin nuts 225g	Chili bean 410g	Spag bol 175g	Jerky 30g
	FD porridge 120g	Muesli bar	Tuna 85g	Tika chicken 90g	Juice conc
		Gum 14g	Salmon 100g	Honey soy chicken 90g	Cordial
		Gingernut 250g	Pasta meal 70g	Satay beef 300g pp	Skim milk 400g
		Bis choc chip 240g	Dol pasta 215g	Hash potato 30g	
		Cashew 40g	Dol tom sc 90g	Mash potato 30g	
		Kitkat 17g		Vege 1	
		Noodles 85g		Vege 2	

	Breakfast	Snack	Lunch	Dinner	Extras
WEEK 4	Light'n'tasty 525g	Gingernut 250g	Mac cheese	Satay beef 300g	Loaf bread
	FD porridge 120g	Wheaten choc 200g	Satay beef pp 300g	Lamb 300g	Full milk pwd 400g
	Scrambled egg 40g	Soup	Chicken 300g	Spag bol 175g	Milo 350g
	FD apple 25g	Noodles 85g	Tuna 85g	Baboyjie 90g	Juice conc
	Milkshake 200g	Raisin nuts 225g	Salmon 100g	Tika chicken 90g	Jerky 15g
		Choc 50g	Can onion steak 400g	Thai chicken 90g	Jerky 25g
		Bar choc 250g	Dol pasta 215g	Honey soy chicken 90g	Jerky 30g
		Cashew 40g	Dol tom sc 90g	Hash potato 30g	Jerky 50g
		Muesli bar	Pasta meal 70g	Mash potato 30g	
			Candy lollies		Vege

NOTES

Use mashed potato to thicken if too much water is added to main meals

There are two servings of potato a week: hash, mash

Porridge: use 120g or ½ cup with hot water to make, add honey, dates

Use cheese sauce, gravy to alter flavor of main meals

FD = Freeze dried

BIBLIOGRAPHY

James Cook, *The Journals*. Prepared from the original manuscripts by J C Beaglehole for the Hakluyt Society, 1955–67. Selected and edited by Philip Edwards, Penguin Books, London, 2003.

Thor Heyerdahl, *Kon Tiki: Across the Pacific by Raft*, translated by F H Lyon, Simon & Schuster Paperbacks, New York, 2013.

Eric Hiscock, *Beyond the West Horizon*, Adlard Coles Limited, London, 1987.

Bernard Moitessier, *The Long Way*, Sheridan House, Dobb's Ferry, NY, 1995.

Joshua Slocum, *Sailing Alone Around the World*, Granada Publishing, London, 1976.

R L Stevenson, *Treasure Island*, Macmillan and Co, London, 1942.